JMP travel guidebooks b

2 to 22 Days in Spain and Portugal
Europe Through the Back Door
Europe 101: History and Art for the Traveler
    (with Gene Openshaw)
Mona Winks: Self-Guided Tours of Europe's Top Museums
    (with Gene Openshaw)
2 to 22 Days in Europe
2 to 22 Days in France (with Steve Smith)
2 to 22 Days in Italy
2 to 22 Days in Great Britain
2 to 22 Days in Germany, Austria & Switzerland
2 to 22 Days in Norway, Sweden & Denmark
Europe Through the Back Door Phrase Books:
    French, Italian, German, and Spanish/Portuguese
Asia Through the Back Door (with Bob Effertz)
Kidding Around Seattle

Rick Steves' company, *Europe Through the Back Door,* provides
many services for budget European travelers, including a free
quarterly newsletter/catalog, budget travel books and accessories,
Eurailpasses (with free video and travel advice included), a free
computer BBS Travel Information Line, a travel partners list,
intimate bus tours of Europe, and a user-friendly Travel Resource
Center in Edmonds, WA. For more information and a free
newsletter subscription, call or write to:

Europe Through the Back Door, Inc.
109 Fourth Avenue N, Box 2009
Edmonds, WA 98020 USA
Tel: 206/771-8303, Fax: 206/771-0833
BBS: 206/771-1902 (1200-2400 baud, 8/N/1)

CONTENTS

CONTENTS

COMBINED SECTONS

Hi, I'm Rick Steves.

I'm the only mono-lingual speaker I know who's had the nerve to design a series of European phrase books. But that's one of the things that makes them better.

You see, after twenty summers of travel through Europe, I've learned first-hand: (1) what's essential for communication in another country, and (2) what's not. I've assembled these essential words and phrases in a logical, no-frills format, and I've worked with native Europeans and seasoned travelers to give you the simplest, clearest translations possible.

But this book is more than just a pocket translator. The words and phrases have been carefully selected to help you have a smarter, smoother trip in Spain and Portugal without going broke. Spain used to be cheap and chaotic. These days it's neither. It's better organized than ever -- and often as expensive as France or Germany. The key to getting more out of every travel dollar is to get closer to the local people, and to rely less on entertainment, restaurants, and hotels that cater only to foreign tourists. This book will not only help you order a meal at a locals-only Sevilla restaurant -- it will also help you discuss politics, social issues and other topics with the family that runs the place. Long after your memories of museums have faded, you'll still treasure the personal encounters you had with your new Iberian friends.

A good phrase book should help you enjoy your Iberian experience -- not just survive it -- so I've added a healthy dose of humor. But please use these phrases carefully, in a self-effacing spirit. Remember that one ugly American can undo the goodwill built by dozens of culturally-sensitive ones.

To get the most out of this book, take the time to internalize and put into practice my Spanish and Portuguese pronunciation tips. Don't worry too much about memorizing grammatical rules, like the gender of a noun; the important thing is to communicate!

You'll notice this book has a tear-out cheat sheet section. Tear it out and keep it in your pocket, so you can easily use it to memorize key words and phrases during otherwise idle moments. You'll also find my *Rolling Rosetta Stone* Word Guide, and special sections on local tongue-twisters, gestures, international words, and tips for using the telephones. As you prepare for your trip, you may want to read this year's edition of my *2 to 22 Days in Spain and Portugal* guidebook.

The Spanish and Portuguese speak less English than their European neighbors. But while the language barrier may seem a little higher, the locals are happy to give an extra boost to any traveler who makes an effort to communicate. If this phrase book helps make that happen, or if you have suggestions for making it better, I'd love to hear from you.

Happy travels,
Rick Steves

Getting Started

Spanish
...opens the door to the land of siestas and fiestas, fun and flamenco. Imported from the Old World throughout the New, Spanish is the most widely spoken romance language in the world. With its straightforward pronunciation, Spanish is also one of the simplest languages to learn.

Here are some tips for pronouncing Spanish words:

C usually sounds like C in cat.
> But *C* followed by *E* or *I* sounds like TH in think.

D sounds like the soft D in soda.

G usually sounds like G in go.
> But *G* followed by *E* or *I* sounds like the guttural J in Baja.

H is silent.

J sounds like the guttural J in Baja.

LL sounds like Y in yes.

Ñ sounds like NI in onion.

R is trrrilled.

V sounds like B in bit.

Z sounds like TH in think.

Spanish vowels:

A sounds like A in father.
E can sound like E in get or AY in play.
I sounds like EE in seed.
O sounds like O in note.
U sounds like OO in moon.

Spanish has a few unusual signs and sounds. The Spanish add extra punctuation to questions and exclamations, like this: *¿Cómo está?* (How are you?) *¡Fantástico!* (Fantastic!) You've probably seen and heard the Spanish *ñ*: think of *señor* and *mañana*. Spanish has a guttural sound similar to the J in Baja California. In the phonetics, the symbol for this clearing-your-throat sound is the italicized *h*.

Spanish words that end in a consonant are stressed on the last syllable, as in *Madrid*. Words ending in a vowel are generally stressed on the second-to-last syllable, as in *amigo*. To override these rules, the Spanish sometimes add an accent mark (´) to the syllable that should be stressed, like this: *rápido* (fast) is pronounced RAH-pee-doh.

When you're speaking a romance language, sex is unavoidable. Even the words are masculine or feminine, and word endings can change depending on gender. A man is *simpático* (friendly), a woman is *simpática*. In this book, we show gender-bender words like this: *simpático[a]*. If you're speaking of a woman (which includes women speaking about themselves), use the *a* ending. It's always pronounced "ah." Words ending in *r*, such as *doctor*, will appear like this: *doctor[a]*. A *doctora* is a female doctor. Words ending in *e*, such as *amable* (kind), apply to either sex.

The endings of Spanish nouns and adjectives agree. Cold weather is *tiempo frío*, and a cold shower is a *ducha fría*.

Plurals are a snap. Add *s* to a word that ends in a vowel, like *pueblo* (village) and *es* to a word that ends in a consonant, like *ciudad* (city). Visit a mix of *pueblos* and *ciudades* to get the full flavor of Spain.

Here's a quick guide to the phonetics we've used in this book:

ah	like A in father.
ar	like AR in park.
ay	like AY in play.
ee	like EE in seed.
eh	like E in get.
ehr	sounds like "air."
g	like G in go.
h	like the guttural J in Baja.
ī	like I in light.

oh	like O in note.
or	like OR in core.
oo	like OO in moon.
ow	like OW in now.
oy	like OY in toy.
s	like S in sun.

In northern and central Spain, Spanish sounds as if it's spoken with a lisp. *Gracias* (thank you) sounds like GRAH-thee-ahs. As you head farther south, you'll notice a difference in pronunciation. In southern Spain, along the coast, people thpeak without the lisp: *Gracias* sounds like GRAH-see-ahs. Listen to and imitate the Spanish people around you.

You'll often hear the Spanish say, *"Por favor"* (Please). The Spanish are friendly, polite people. Use *por favor* whenever you can and you'll make friends wherever you go.

Spanish Basics

Meeting and greeting the Spanish:

Hello.	**Hola.**	OH-lah
Good morning.	**Buenos días.**	BWAY-nohs DEE-ahs
Good afternoon.	**Buenas tardes.**	BWAY-nahs TAR-days
Good evening.	**Buenas tardes.**	BWAY-nahs TAR-days
Mr.	**Señor**	sayn-YOR
Mrs.	**Señora**	sayn-YOH-rah
Miss	**Señorita**	sayn-yoh-REE-tah
How are you?	**¿Cómo está?**	KOH-moh ays-TAH
Very well, thanks.	**Muy bien, gracias.**	MOO-ee bee-YEHN GRAH-thee-ahs
And you?	**¿Y usted?**	ee oos-TEHD
My name is...	**Me llamo...**	may YAH-moh
What's your name?	**¿Cómo se llama?**	KOH-moh say YAH-mah
Pleased to meet you.	**Mucho gusta.**	MOO-choh GOO-stah
Where are you from?	**¿De dónde es usted?**	day DOHN-day ays oos-TEHD
I am... / Are you...?	**Estoy... / ¿Está usted...?**	ays-TOY / ays-TAH oos-TEHD
...on vacation	**...de vacaciones**	day bah-kah-thee-OH-nays
...on business	**...de negocios**	day nay-GOH-thee-ohs
See you later.	**Hasta luego.**	AH-stah loo-AY-goh

Goodbye.	**Adiós.**	ah-dee-OHS
Good luck!	**¡Buena suerte!**	BWAY-nah SWEHR-tay
Have a good trip!	**¡Buen viaje!**	bwayn bee-AH-_hay_

The top 50 survival phrases

Yes, you can survive in Spain using only these phrases. Many are repeated on your tear-out cheat sheet near the end of this book.

The ten essentials:

Hello.	**Hola.**	OH-lah
Do you speak English?	**¿Habla usted inglés?**	AH-blah oos-TEHD een-GLAYS
Yes.	**Sí.**	see
No.	**No.**	noh
I don't understand.	**No comprendo.**	noh kohm-PREHN-doh
I'm sorry.	**Lo siento.**	loh see-EHN-toh
Please.	**Por favor.**	por fah-BOR
Thanks.	**Gracias.**	GRAH-thee-ahs
Thank you very much.	**Muchas gracias.**	MOO-chahs GRAH-thee-ahs
Goodbye.	**Adiós.**	ah-dee-OHS

Where?

Where is a...?	**Donde hay un...?**	DOHN-day ī oon
...hotel	**...hotel**	oh-TEL
...youth hostel	**...albergue de juventud**	ahl-BEHR-gay day *h*oo-behn-TOOD
...restaurant	**...restaurante**	rays-toh-RAHN-tay
...grocery store	**...supermercado**	soo-pehr-mehr-KAH-doh
Where is the...?	**Dónde está la...?**	DOHN-day ays-TAH lah
...train station	**...estación de trenes**	ays-tah-thee-OHN day TRAY-nays
...tourist information office	**...Oficina de Turismo**	oh-fee-THEE-nah day too-REES-moh
Where are the toilets?	**¿Dónde están los servicios?**	DOHN-day ays-TAHN lohs sehr-BEE-thee-ohs
men / women	**hombres / mujeres**	OHM-brays / moo-*H*EH-rays

How much?

How much does it cost?	**¿Cuánto cuesta?**	KWAHN-toh KWAYS-tah
Will you write it down?	**¿Me lo puede escribir?**	may loh PWAY-day ays-kree-BEER
Cheap.	**Barato.**	bah-RAH-toh
Cheaper.	**Más barato.**	mahs bah-RAH-toh

Is it included?	**¿Está incluido?**	ays-TAH een-kloo-EE-doh
I would like...	**Quería...**	keh-REE-ah
We would like...	**Queríamos...**	keh-REE-ah-mohs
Just a little.	**Un poquito.**	oon poh-KEE-toh
More.	**Más.**	mahs
A ticket.	**Un billete.**	oon bee-YEH-tay
A room.	**Una habitación.**	OO-nah ah-bee-tah-thee-OHN
The bill.	**La cuenta.**	lah KWAYN-tah

Number crunching:

one	**uno**	OO-noh
two	**dos**	dohs
three	**tres**	trays
four	**cuatro**	KWAH-troh
five	**cinco**	THEEN-koh
six	**seis**	says
seven	**siete**	see-EH-tay
eight	**ocho**	OH-choh
nine	**nueve**	NWAY-bay
ten	**diez**	dee-AYTH

Moving on:

I go to...	**Voy a...**	boy ah
We go to...	**Vamos a...**	BAH-mohs ah
today	**hoy**	oy
tomorrow	**mañana**	mahn-YAH-nah
departure	**salida**	sah-LEE-dah
At what time?	**¿A qué hora?**	ah kay OH-rah

What's up:

Excuse me. (to get attention)	**Perdón.**	pehr-DOHN
Just a moment.	**Un momento.**	oon moh-MEHN-toh
It's a problem.	**Es un problema.**	ays oon proh-BLAY-mah
Very good.	**Muy bien.**	MOO-ee bee-YEHN
Fantastic!	**¡Fantástico!**	fahn-TAHS-tee-koh
You are very kind.	**Usted es muy amable.**	oos-TEHD ays MOO-ee ah-MAH-blay

Be creative. You can combine these 50 survival phrases to say: "Two, please," or "No, thank you," or "I'd like a cheap hotel," or "Cheaper, please?" Please is a magic word in any language. If you want something and you don't know the word for it, just point and say, *"Por favor"* (Please).

Struggling with Spanish:

Do you speak English?	¿Habla usted inglés?	AH-blah oos-TEHD een-GLAYS
Even a teeny weeny bit?	¿Ni un poquito?	nee oon poh-KEE-toh
Please speak English.	Hable en inglés, por favor.	AH-blay ayn een-GLAYS por fah-BOR
You speak English well.	Usted habla bien el inglés.	oos-TEHD AH-blah bee-YEHN ehl een-GLAYS
I don't speak Spanish.	No hablo español.	noh AH-bloh ays-pahn-YOHL
I speak a little Spanish.	Hablo un poco de español.	AH-bloh oon POH-koh day ays-pahn-YOHL
I speak ten words in Spanish.	Solo sé diez palabras en español.	SOH-loh say dee-AYTH pah-LAH-brahs ayn ays-pahn-YOHL
I study Spanish.	Estudio español.	ays-TOO-dee-oh ays-pahn-YOHL
Excuse...	Perdón por...	pehr-DOHN por
Correct...	Corrija...	kor-REE-hah
...my pronunciation.	...mi pronunciación.	mee proh-noon-thee-ah-thee-OHN
What is this in Spanish?	¿Cómo se dice esto en español?	KOH-moh say DEE-thay AYS-toh ayn ays-pahn-YOHL
Excuse me? (didn't hear)	¿Puede repetir?	PWAY-day ray-pay-TEER

Repeat.	**Repita.**	ray-PEE-tah
Speak slowly.	**Hable despacio.**	AH-blay day-SPAH-thee-oh
Do you understand?	**¿Comprende?**	kohm-PREHN-day
I understand.	**Comprendo.**	kohm-PREHN-doh
I don't understand.	**No comprendo.**	noh kohm-PREHN-doh
Will you write it down?	**¿Me lo puede escribir?**	may loh PWAY-day ays-kree-BEER
Does anybody here speak English?	**¿Habla alguien inglés?**	AH-blah AHL-gee-ehn een-GLAYS

Common questions in Spanish:

How much?	**¿Cuánto?**	KWAHN-toh
How many?	**¿Cuánto?**	KWAHN-toh
How long? (time)	**¿Cuánto tiempo?**	KWAHN-toh tee-EHM-poh
How far?	**¿A qué distancia?**	ah kay dees-TAHN-thee-ah
How?	**¿Cómo?**	KOH-moh
Is it possible?	**¿Es posible?**	ays poh-SEE-blay
What?	**¿Qué?**	kay
What is that?	**¿Qué es esto?**	kay ays AYS-toh
What is better?	**¿Qué es mejor?**	kay ays may-HOR
When?	**¿Cuándo?**	KWAHN-doh
What time is it?	**¿Qué hora es?**	kay OH-rah ays
At what time?	**¿A qué hora?**	ah kay OH-rah

What time does this...?	**¿A qué hora...?**	ah kay OH-rah
...open	**...abren**	AH-brehn
...close	**...cierran**	thee-AY-rahn
Do you have...?	**¿Tiene...?**	tee-EHN-ay
Where is...?	**¿Dónde está...?**	DOHN-day ays-TAH
Where are...?	**¿Dónde están...?**	DOHN-day ays-TAHN
Who?	**¿Quién?**	kee-EHN
Why?	**¿Por qué?**	por kay
Why not?	**¿Por qué no?**	por kay noh

Even a single word can turn into a question if you ask it in a questioning tone. A simple way to ask, "Where are the toilets?" is to say, "*¿Servicios?*"

Spanish names for places:

Spain	**España**	ays-PAHN-yah
Madrid	**Madrid**	mah-DREED
Seville	**Sevilla**	seh-VEE-yah
Portugal	**Portugal**	por-too-GAHL
Lisbon	**Lisboa**	lees-BOH-ah
Morocco	**Marruecos**	mar-WAY-kohs
France	**Francia**	FRAHN-thee-ah
Germany	**Alemania**	ah-lay-MAHN-yah
United States	**Estados Unidos**	ays-TAH-dohs oo-NEE-dohs
the world	**el mundo**	ehl MOON-doh

Yin and yang:

cheap / expensive	**barato / caro**	bah-RAH-toh / KAH-roh
big / small	**grande / pequeño**	GRAHN-day / pay-KAYN-yoh
hot / cold	**caliente / frío**	kahl-YEHN-tay / FREE-oh
open / closed	**abierto / cerrado**	ah-bee-YEHR-toh / thehr-RAH-doh
entrance / exit	**entrada / salida**	ayn-TRAH-dah / sah-LEE-dah
arrive / depart	**llegar / salir**	yay-GAR / sah-LEER
early / late	**temprano / tarde**	tehm-PRAH-noh / TAR-day
soon / later	**pronto / más tarde**	PROHN-toh / mahs TAR-day
fast / slow	**rápido / despacio**	RAH-pee-doh / day-SPAH-thee-oh
here / there	**aquí / allí**	ah-KEE / ah-YEE
near / far	**cerca / lejos**	THEHR-kah / LAY-hohs
good / bad	**bueno / malo**	BWAY-noh / MAH-loh
best / worst	**mejor / peor**	may-HOR / pay-OR
a little / lots	**un poco / mucho**	oon POH-koh / MOO-choh
more / less	**más / menos**	mahs / MAY-nohs
easy / difficult	**fácil / difícil**	FAH-theel / dee-FEE-theel
beautiful / ugly	**bonito / feo**	boh-NEE-toh / FAY-oh

smart / stupid	**listo / estúpido**	LEE-stoh / ays-TOO-pee-doh
vacant / occupied	**libre / ocupado**	LEE-bray / oh-koo-PAH-doh
with / without	**con / sin**	kohn / seen

Little words that are big in Spain:

I	**yo**	yoh
you (formal)	**usted**	oos-TEHD
you (informal)	**tú**	too
he	**él**	ehl
she	**ella**	AY-yah
we	**nosotros**	noh-SOH-trohs
and	**y**	ee
at	**a**	ah
but	**pero**	PAY-roh
by (via)	**por**	por
for	**para**	PAH-rah
from	**de**	day
not	**no**	noh
now	**ahora**	ah-OH-rah
only	**solo**	SOH-loh
or	**o**	oh
this	**esto**	AYS-toh
to	**a**	ah
very	**muy**	MOO-ee

Numbers

0	cero	THEHR-oh
1	uno	OO-noh
2	dos	dohs
3	tres	trays
4	cuatro	KWAH-troh
5	cinco	THEEN-koh
6	seis	says
7	siete	see-EH-tay
8	ocho	OH-choh
9	nueve	NWAY-bay
10	diez	dee-AYTH
11	once	OHN-thay
12	doce	DOH-thay
13	trece	TRAY-thay
14	catorce	kah-TOR-thay
15	quince	KEEN-thay
16	dieciséis	dee-ay-thee-SAYS
17	diecisiete	dee-ay-thee-see-EH-tay
18	dieciocho	dee-ay-thee-OH-choh
19	diecinueve	dee-ay-thee-NWAY-bay
20	veinte	BAYN-tay
21	veintiuno	bayn-tee-OO-noh
22	veintidós	bayn-tee-DOHS
23	veintitrés	bayn-tee-TRAYS
30	treinta	TRAYN-tah
31	treinta y uno	TRAYN-tah ee OO-noh

40	**cuarenta**	kwah-REHN-tah
41	**cuarenta y uno**	kwah-REHN-tah ee OO-noh
50	**cincuenta**	theen-KWEHN-tah
60	**sesenta**	say-SEHN-tah
70	**setenta**	say-TEHN-tah
80	**ochenta**	oh-CHEHN-tah
90	**noventa**	noh-BEHN-tah
100	**cien**	thee-EHN
101	**ciento uno**	thee-EHN-toh OO-noh
102	**ciento dos**	thee-EHN-toh dohs
143	**ciento cuarenta y tres**	thee-EHN-toh kwar-REHN-tah ee trays
200	**doscientos**	dohs-thee-EHN-tohs
1000	**mil**	meel
1994	**mil novecientos noventa y cuatro**	meel noh-bay-thee-EHN-tohs noh-BEHN-tah ee KWAH-troh
2000	**dos mil**	dohs meel
10,000	**diez mil**	dee-AYTH meel
1,000,000	**millón**	mee-YOHN
first	**primero**	pree-MAY-roh
second	**segundo**	say-GOON-doh
third	**tercero**	tehr-THEHR-oh
half	**mitad**	mee-TAHD
fifty percent	**cincuenta por ciento**	theen-KWEHN-tah por thee-EHN-toh
number one	**número uno**	NOO-may-roh OO-noh

Money

Handy Spanish money words:

bank	**banco**	BAHN-koh
money	**dinero**	dee-NAY-roh
change money	**cambio de moneda**	KAHM-bee-oh day moh-NAY-dah
exchange	**cambio**	KAHM-bee-oh
traveler's check	**cheque de viajero**	CHAY-kay day bee-ah-HAY-roh
credit card	**tarjeta de crédito**	tar-HAY-tah day KRAY-dee-toh
cash advance	**adelanto de dinero**	ah-day-LAHN-toh day dee-NAY-roh
transfer of money	**transferencia**	trahns-fay-REHN-thee-ah
cash machine	**caja automática**	KAH-hah ow-toh-MAH-tee-kah
cashier	**cajero**	KAH-hehr-oh
receipt	**recibo**	ray-THEE-boh

There are about 110 pesetas to the dollar, so pesetas are close to being pennies. To figure out Spanish prices in dollars, cover the last two zeros and subtract about 10%. A price of 2000 pesetas equals roughly $18.

Changing money in Spain:

Can you change dollars?	¿Me puede cambiar dólares?	may PWAY-day kahm-bee-AR DOH-lah-rays
What is your exchange rate for dollars...?	¿A cuanto pagan el dólar...?	ah KWAHN-toh PAH-gahn ehl DOH-lar
...in traveler's checks	...en cheques de viajero	ayn CHAY-kays day bee-ah-*HAY*-roh
Are there extra fees?	¿Tiene cuotas extras?	tee-EHN-ay KWOH-tahs AYK-strahs
What is...?	¿Cuánto es...?	KWAHN-toh ays
...the service charge	...el cobro de servicio	ehl KOH-broh day sehr-BEE-thee-oh
...the commission	...la comisión	lah koh-mee-see-OHN
I would like...	Quería...	keh-REE-ah
...small bills.	...billetes pequeños.	bee-YEH-tays pay-KAYN-yohs
...large bills.	...billetes grandes.	bee-YEH-tays GRAHN-days
...coins.	...monedas.	mon-NAY-dahs
I think you've made a mistake.	Creo que se confundió.	KRAY-oh kay say kohn-foon-dee-OH
I'm broke.	No tengo dinero.	noh TAYN-goh dee-NAY-roh
I'm poor.	Soy pobre.	soy POH-bray
I'm rich.	Soy rico[a].	soy REE-koh

Public Transportation

Tickets:

ticket	**billete**	bee-YEH-tay
ticket office	**venta de billetes**	BAYN-tah day bee-YEH-tays
schedule	**horario**	oh-RAH-ree-oh
one way	**de ida**	day EE-dah
roundtrip	**ida y vuelta**	EE-dah ee BWEHL-tah
overnight	**durante la noche**	doo-RAHN-tay lah NOH-chay
direct	**directo**	dee-REHK-toh
connection	**enlace**	ayn-LAH-thay
express service	**expreso**	ayk-SPRAY-soh
first class	**primera clase**	pree-MAY-rah KLAH-say
second class	**segunda clase**	say-GOON-dah KLAH-say
reservation	**reserva**	ray-SEHR-bah
seat...	**asiento...**	ah-see-EHN-toh
...window	**...con ventana**	kohn bayn-TAH-nah
...aisle	**...cerca pasillo**	THEHR-kah pah-SEE-yoh
non-smoking	**no fumadores**	noh foo-mah-DOH-rays
refund	**devolución**	day-voh-loo-thee-OHN

At the station:

arrival	**llegada**	yay-GAH-dah
departure	**salida**	sah-LEE-dah
delay	**retraso**	ray-TRAH-soh
waiting room	**sala de espera**	SAH-lah day ays-PAY-rah
lockers	**casilleros**	kah-see-YAY-rohs
baggage	**maletas**	mah-LAY-tahs
baggage check room	**oficina de equipaje**	oh-fee-THEE-nah day ay-kee-PAH-*h*ay
lost and found office	**oficina de objetos perdidos**	oh-fee-THEE-nah day ohb-*H*AY-tohs pehr-DEE-dohs
tourist information office	**Oficina de Turismo**	oh-fee-THEE-nah day too-REES-moh

Trains:

Spanish Railways	**R.E.N.F.E.**	REHN-fay
train station	**estación de tren**	ays-tah-thee-OHN day trayn
train information	**información de trenes**	een-for-mah-thee-OHN day TRAY-nays
train	**tren**	trayn
high-speed train	**Talgo**	TAHL-goh
to the platforms	**en los andenes**	ayn lohs AHN-deh-nays
platform	**andén**	ahn-DAYN

track	**vía**	BEE-ah
train car	**vagón**	bah-GOHN
dining car	**coche comedor**	KOH-chay koh-may-DOR
sleeper car	**coche cama**	KOH-chay KAH-mah
sleeper berth	**litera**	LEE-tay-rah
conductor	**conductor**	kohn-dook-TOR

Spanish trains require reservations for longer trips
(even if you have a Eurailpass and the train is empty).
When you arrive in a town, make your out-bound
reservation right away. The downtown RENFE office
is often more efficient at making reservations than the
train station.

Buses:

bus station	**estación de autobuses**	ays-tah-thee-OHN day ow-toh-BOOS-ays
long-distance bus	**autocar**	ow-toh-KAR
city bus	**autobús interurbano**	ow-toh-BOOS een-tehr-oor-BAH-noh
bus stop	**parada de autobus**	pah-RAH-dah day ow-toh-BOOS

Buses connect many smaller Spanish towns better and
cheaper than the trains. Tourist information offices
have inter- and intra-city bus schedules.

Spanish transportation phrases:

How much is the fare to...?	¿Cuánto cuesta el billete a...?	KWAHN-toh KWAYS-tah ehl bee-YEH-tay ah
I'd like...	Quería...	keh-REE-ah
...to go to ___.	...ir a ___.	eer ah
...a ticket to ___.	...un billete para ___.	oon bee-YEH-tay PAH-rah
Is a reservation required?	¿Se requiere una reserva?	say ray-kee-EH-ray OO-nah ray-SEHR-bah
I'd like to leave...	Quería salir...	keh-REE-ah sah-LEER
I'd like to arrive...	Quería llegar...	keh-REE-ah yay-GAR
...by ___. (fill in time)	...a las ___.	ah lahs
...in the morning.	...por la mañana.	por lah mahn-YAH-nah
...in the afternoon.	...por la tarde.	por lah TAR-day
...in the evening.	...por la noche.	por lah NOH-chay
Is there...?	¿Hay...?	ī
...an earlier departure	...una salida más temprana	OO-nah sah-LEE-dah mahs tehm-PRAH-nah
...a later departure	...una salida más tarde	OO-nah sah-LEE-dah mahs TAR-day
...a supplement	...un suplemento	oon soo-play-MEHN-toh
...a cheaper ticket	...un billete más barato	oon bee-YEH-tay mahs bah-RAH-toh
When is the next departure?	¿Cuándo es la siguiente salida?	KWAHN-doh ays lah seeg-ee-EHN-tay sah-LEE-dah

Will you write it down?	**¿Me lo puede escribir?**	may loh PWAY-day ays-kree-BEER
Where does it leave from?	**¿De dónde sale?**	day DOHN-day SAH-lay
On what track?	**¿En qué vía?**	ayn kay BEE-ah
When will it arrive?	**¿Cuándo tiene su llegada?**	KWAHN-doh tee-EHN-ay soo yay-GAH-dah
Is it direct?	**¿Es directo?**	ays dee-REHK-toh
Must I transfer?	**¿Tengo que cambiar?**	TAYN-goh kay kahm-bee-AR
When? / Where?	**¿Cuándo? / ¿Dónde?**	KWAHN-doh / DOHN-day
Which train to...?	**¿Qué tren para...?**	kay trayn PAH-rah
Which train car to...?	**¿Qué vagón para...?**	kay bah-GOHN PAH-rah
Which bus to...?	**¿Qué autocar para...?**	kay ow-toh-CAR PAH-rah
Does it stop at...?	**¿Para en....?**	PAH-rah ayn
Is this (seat) free?	**¿Está libre?**	ays-TAH LEE-bray
Save my place.	**Guardeme mi asiento.**	GWAR-deh-may mee ah-see-EHN-toh
Where are you going?	**¿A dónde va?**	ah DOHN-day vah
I go to...	**Voy a...**	boy ah
Can you tell me when to get off?	**¿Me puede decir cuando me tengo que bajar?**	may PWAY-day day-THEER KWAHN-doh may TAYN-goh kay bah-HAR

Reading Spanish train and bus schedules:

a	to
desde	from
diario	daily
días	days
días de semana	weekdays
domingo	Sunday
domingos y festivos	Sunday and holidays
excepto	except
festivos	holiday
hasta	until
llegadas	arrival
sábado	Saturday
salidas	departure
solo	only
todos	every

Spanish schedules use the 24-hour clock. It's like American time until noon. After that, subtract twelve and add p.m. So 13:00 is 1 p.m. and 19:00 is 7 p.m. Midnight is 24:00. If your train is scheduled to depart at 00:01, it will leave one minute after midnight.

Taking taxis in Spain:

taxi	**taxi**	TAHK-see
Where is a taxi stand?	**¿Dónde está la parada de taxi?**	DOHN-day ays-TAH lah pah-RAH-dah day TAHK-see
Are you free?	**¿Está libre?**	ays-TAH LEE-bray
Occupied.	**Ocupado.**	oh-koo-PAH-doh
How much will it cost to go to...?	**¿Cuánto me costará ir a...?**	KWAHN-toh may koh-stah-RAH eer ah
Too much.	**Demasiado.**	day-mah-see-AH-doh
How many people can you take?	**¿A cuánta gente puede llevar?**	ah KWAHN-tah HEHN-tay PWAY-day yay-BAR
Is there an extra fee?	**¿Hay una tarifa extra?**	ī OO-nah tah-REE-fah AYK-strah
The meter, please.	**El taxímetro, por favor.**	ehl tahk-SEE-may-troh por fah-BOR
The most direct route.	**La ruta más directa.**	lah ROO-tah mahs dee-REHK-tah
Slow down.	**Más despacio.**	mahs day-SPAH-thee-oh
If you don't slow down, I'll throw up.	**Si no va más despacio, voy a vomitar.**	see noh bah mahs day-SPAH-thee-oh boy ah boh-mee-TAR
Stop here.	**Pare aquí.**	PAH-ray ah-KEE
Can you wait?	**¿Puede esperar?**	PWAY-day ays-pay-RAR

I'll never forget this ride.	**Nunca me voy a olvidar de este recorrido.**	NOON-kah may boy ah ohl-bee-DAR day AYS-tay ray-koh-REE-doh
Where did you learn to drive?	**¿Dónde aprendió a conducir?**	DOHN-day ah-prehn-dee-OH ah kohn-doo-THEER
I'll only pay what's on the meter.	**Solo voy a pagar lo que dice el taxímetro.**	SOH-loh boy ah pah-GAR loh kay DEE-thay ehl tahk-SEE-may-troh
My change, please.	**Mí cambio, por favor.**	mee KAHM-bee-oh por fah-BOR
Keep the change.	**Quédese con el cambio.**	KAY-day-say kohn ehl KAHM-bee-oh

Taxis in Spain are reasonable, except for going to and from airports (use local buses for these trips). If you have trouble flagging down a taxi, ask for directions to a taxi stand. For an alternative to taxis in Madrid or Barcelona, try the subway. Look for *metro* signs.

Driving

Wheeling and dealing:

I'd like to rent...	**Quería alquilar...**	keh-REE-ah ahl-kee-LAR
...a car.	**...un coche.**	oon KOH-chay
...a motorcyle.	**...una moto.**	OO-nah MOH-toh
...a motor scooter.	**...una motocicleta.**	OO-nah moh-toh-thee-KLAY-tah
...a bicycle.	**...una bicicleta.**	OO-nah bee-thee-KLAY-tah
...a secluded beach.	**...una playa insólita.**	OO-nah PLĪ-yah een-SOH-lee-tah
How much per...?	**¿Cuánto es por...?**	KWAHN-toh ays por
...hour	**...hora**	OH-rah
...day	**...día**	DEE-ah
...week	**...semana**	say-MAH-nah

Gassing up in Spain:

gas station	**gasolinera**	gah-soh-lee-NAY-rah
The nearest gas station?	**¿La gasolinera más cercana?**	lah gah-soh-lee-NAY-rah mahs thehr-KAH-nah
Is it self-service?	**¿Es auto-servicio?**	ays ow-toh-sehr-BEE-thee-oh

Fill the tank.	**Llene el depósito.**	YAY-nay ehl day-POH-see-toh
I need...	**Necesito...**	nay-thay-SEE-toh
...gas.	**...gasolina.**	gah-soh-LEE-nah
...unleaded.	**...sin plomo.**	seen PLOH-moh
...regular.	**...normal.**	nor-MAHL
...super.	**...super.**	soo-PEHR
...diesel.	**...diesel.**	DEE-sehl
Check...	**Cheque...**	CHAY-kay
...the oil.	**...el aceite.**	ehl ah-THAY-tay
...the air in the tires.	**...el aire en las ruedas.**	ehl Ī-ray ayn lahs roo-AY-dahs
...the water.	**...el agua.**	ehl AH-gwah
...the radiator.	**...el radiador.**	ehl rah-dee-ah-DOR
...the battery.	**...la batería.**	lah bah-tay-REE-ah
...the fuses.	**...los fusibles.**	lohs foo-SEE-blays
...the fanbelt.	**...la correa del ventilador.**	lah koh-RAY-ah dayl bayn-tee-lah-DOR
...the brakes.	**...los frenos.**	lohs FRAY-nohs
...my pulse.	**...mi pulso.**	mee POOL-soh

Rather than dollars and gallons, gas pumps in Spain will read pesetas and liters (roughly 110 pesetas in a dollar, and 4 liters in a gallon).

Spanish car trouble:

accident	**accidente**	ahk-thee-DEHN-tay
breakdown	**averiado**	ah-bay-ree-AH-doh
funny noise	**ruido extraño**	roo-EE-doh ayk-STRAHN-yoh
electrical problem	**problema eléctrico**	proh-BLAY-mah ay-LEHK-tree-koh
My car won't start.	**Mi coche no enciende.**	mee KOH-chay noh ayn-thee-EHN-day
This doesn't work.	**Esto no funciona.**	AYS-toh noh foonk-thee-OH-nah
It's overheating.	**Está caliente.**	ays-TAH kahl-YEHN-tay
I need...	**Necesito...**	nay-thay-SEE-toh
...a tow truck.	**...una grúa.**	OO-nah GROO-ah
...a mechanic.	**...un mecánico.**	oon may-KAH-nee-koh
...a stiff drink.	**...un trago.**	oon TRAH-goh
Can you fix it?	**¿Lo puede arreglar?**	loh PWAY-day ah-ray-GLAR
Just do the essentials.	**Haga solo lo esencial.**	AH-gah SOH-loh loh ay-sehn-thee-AHL
When will it be ready?	**¿Cuándo estará listo?**	KWAHN-doh ays-tah-RAH LEE-stoh
How much will it cost to make it run?	**¿Cuánto costará el mínimo arreglo?**	KWAHN-toh koh-stah-RAH ehl MEE-nee-moh ah-RAY-gloh
I'm going to faint.	**Me voy a desmayar.**	may boy ah dehs-mah-YAR

Parking in Spain:

parking garage	**estacionamiento**	ays-tah-thee-oh-nah-mee-EHN-toh
Where can I park?	**¿Dónde puedo aparcar?**	DOHN-day PWAY-doh ah-par-KAR
Is parking nearby?	**¿Hay un estacionamiento cercano?**	ī oon ays-tah-thee-oh-nah-mee-EHN-toh thehr-KAHN-noh
Can I park here?	**¿Puedo aparcar aquí?**	PWAY-doh ah-par-KAR ah-KEE
How long can I park here?	**¿Por cuánto tiempo puedo aparcar aquí?**	por KWAHN-toh tee-EHM-poh PWAY-doh ah-par-KAR ah-KEE
Must I pay to park here?	**¿Tengo que pagar por aparcar aquí?**	TAYN-goh kay pah-GAR por ah-par-KAR ah-KEE
Is this a safe place to park?	**¿Es este un sitio seguro para aparcar?**	ays AYS-tay oon SEE-tee-oh say-GOO-roh PAH-rah ah-par-KAR

Parking in Spain can be hazardous. Park legally. Many towns require parking permits, sold at tobacco shops. To give your car a local profile, cover the rental decal and put a local newspaper inside the back window. Leave the car empty and, some would advise, unlocked overnight. If it's a hatchback, remove the shelf behind the back seat to show thieves you have *nada* in the trunk. Get safe parking tips from your hotel.

Spanish bike bits:

Can I take a bicycle...?	**¿Puedo llevar mi bicicleta...?**	PWAY-doh yay-BAR mee bee-thee-KLAY-tah
...on the train	**...en el tren**	ayn ehl trayn
...on the bus	**...en el autobús**	ayn ehl ow-toh-BOOS
...on the boat	**...en el barco**	ayn ehl BAR-koh
Do I load it myself?	**¿Debo de cargarla solo[a]?**	DAY-boh day kar-GAR-lah SOH-loh
Can you fix my...?	**¿Puede arreglarme mi...?**	PWAY-day ah-ray-GLAR-may mee
...bicycle	**...bicicleta**	bee-thee-KLAY-tah
...tire	**...neumático**	new-MAH-tee-koh
...inner tube	**...cámara de aire**	KAH-mah-rah day Ī-ray
...wheel	**...rueda**	roo-AY-dah
...spoke	**...radio**	RAH-dee-oh
...chain	**...cadena**	kah-DAY-nah
...shifter	**...palanca**	pah-LAHN-kah
...brakes	**...frenos**	FRAY-nohs
I brake for bakeries.	**Paro en cada panadería.**	PAH-roh ayn KAH-dah pah-nah-deh-REE-ah

Finding Your Way

Key Spanish navigation words:

straight	**derecho**	day-RAY-choh
left / right	**izquierda / derecha**	eeth-KEHR-dah / day-RAY-chah
first / next	**primero / siguiente**	pree-MAY-roh / seeg-ee-EHN-tay
intersection	**intersección**	een-tehr-sehk-thee-OHN
stoplight	**semáforo**	say-MAH-foh-roh
square	**plaza**	PLAH-thah
street	**calle**	KAH-yay
bridge	**puente**	PWEHN-tay
tunnel	**túnel**	TOO-nehl
overpass	**paso superior**	PAH-soh soo-pehr-ee-OR
underpass	**paso inferior**	PAH-soh een-fehr-ee-OR
highway	**carretera**	kah-ray-TAY-rah
freeway	**autopista**	ow-toh-PEE-stah
map	**mapa**	MAH-pah

Getting directions in Spain:

I go to...	**Voy a...**	boy ah
How do I get to...?	**¿Cómo llego a...?**	KOH-moh YAY-goh ah
How many minutes...?	**¿Cuánto tiempo...?**	KWAHN-toh tee-EHM-poh
...on foot	**...a pié**	ah pee-AY
...by car	**...en coche**	ayn KOH-chay
How many kilometers to...?	**¿Cuántos kilómetros a...?**	KWAHN-tohs kee-LOH-may-trohs ah
What's the... route to Tossa?	**¿Cuál es el... camino para Tossa?**	kwahl ays ehl... kah-MEE-noh PAH-rah TOH-sah
...best	**...mejor**	may-HOR
...fastest	**...más rápido**	mahs RAH-pee-doh
...most interesting	**...más interesante**	mahs een-tay-ray-SAHN-tay
Show me on this map.	**Indíqueme en el mapa.**	een-DEE-kay-may ayn ehl MAH-pah
I'm lost.	**Estoy perdido[a].**	ays-TOY pehr-DEE-doh
Where am I?	**¿Dónde estoy?**	DOHN-day ays-TOY
Who am I?	**¿Quién soy?**	kee-EHN soy
Where is...?	**¿Dónde está...?**	DOHN-day ays-TAH
The nearest...?	**¿El más cercano...?**	ehl mahs thehr-KAH-noh
Where is this address?	**¿Dónde se encuentra esta dirección?**	DOHN-day say ayn-KWEHN-trah AYS-tah dee-rehk-thee-OHN

Reading Spanish road signs:

ceda el paso	yield
centro de la ciudad	to the center of town
cuidado	caution
despacio	slow
desvío	detour
dirección única	one-way street
entrada	entrance
estacionamiento prohibido	no parking
obras	workers ahead
salida	exit
peatones	pedestrians
stop	stop

The flashing lights of a patrol car are a sure sign that someone is in trouble. If it's you, remember this handy phrase: *"Lo siento, soy un turista."* (Sorry, I'm a tourist.)

Other Spanish signs you may bump into:

abierto	open
abierto de... a...	open from... to...
agua no potable	undrinkable water
alquilo	for rent
caballeros	men
cerrado	closed
cerrado por vacaciones	closed for vacation
cerrado por obras	closed for restoration
entrada libre	free admission
no fumar	no smoking
no tocar	do not touch
ocupado	occupied
paso prohibido	no entry
peligro	danger
prohibido	forbidden
salida de emergencia	emergency exit
señoras	women
servicios	toilets
Turismo	tourist information office
vendo	for sale

Telephones

Key Spanish telephone words:

telephone office	**Telefónica**	tay-lay-FOH-nee-kah
telephone	**teléfono**	tay-LAY-foh-noh
operator	**telefonista**	tay-lay-foh-NEE-stah
international assistance	**asistencia internacional**	ah-see-STEHN-thee-ah een-tehr-nah-thee-oh-NAHL
country code	**prefijo del país**	pray-FEE-hoh dayl pah-EES
area code	**prefijo**	pray-FEE-hoh
phone card	**tarjeta telefónica**	tar-HAY-tah tay-lay-FOH-nee-kah
telephone book	**guía de teléfonos**	GEE-ah day tay-LAY-foh-nohs
yellow pages	**páginas amarillas**	PAH-hee-nahs ah-mah-REE-yahs
toll-free call	**llamada gratuita**	yah-MAH-dah grah-TWEE-tah
out of service	**averiado**	ah-bay-ree-AH-doh

Handy Spanish phone phrases:

The nearest phone?	**¿El teléfono más cercano?**	ehl tay-LAY-foh-noh mahs thehr-KAH-noh
It doesn't work.	**No funciona.**	noh foonk-thee-OH-nah
Where is the telephone office?	**¿Dónde está la Telefónica?**	DOHN-day ays-TAH lah tay-lay-FOH-nee-kah
I'd like to telephone... ...the United States.	**Quería llamar... ...a los Estados Unidos.**	keh-REE-ah yah-MAR ah lohs ays-TAH-dohs oo-NEE-dohs
How much per minute?	**¿Cuánto es por minuto?**	KWAHN-toh ays por mee-NOO-toh
I'd like to make a... call.	**Quería hacer una llamada...**	keh-REE-ah ah-THEHR OO-nah yah-MAH-dah
...local	**...local.**	loh-KAHL
...collect	**...a cobro revertido.**	ah KOH-broh ray-behr-TEE-doh
...credit card	**...con tarjeta.**	kohn tar-*HAY*-tah
...person to person	**...de persona a persona.**	day pehr-SOH-nah ah pehr-SOH-nah
...long distance (within Spain)	**...nacional.**	nah-thee-oh-NAHL
...international	**...internacional.**	een-tehr-nah-thee-oh-NAHL
...fax	**...fax.**	"fax"

May I use your phone?	**¿Puedo usar su teléfono?**	PWAY-doh oo-SAR soo tay-LAY-foh-noh
Can you dial for me?	**¿Puede marcarme el número?**	PWAY-day mar-KAR-may ehl NOO-may-roh
Can you talk for me?	**¿Puede hablar usted por mi?**	PWAY-day ah-BLAR oos-TEHD por mee
It's busy.	**Está comunicando.**	ays-TAH koh-moo-nee-KAHN-doh
Will you try again?	**¿Llamará otra vez?**	yay-mah-RAH OH-trah bayth
My name is...	**Me llamo...**	may YAH-moh
My number is...	**Mi número es...**	mee NOO-may-roh ays
Speak slowly and clearly.	**Hable despacio y claro.**	AH-blay day-SPAH-thee-oh ee KLAH-roh
Wait a moment.	**Un momento.**	oon moh-MEHN-toh
Don't hang up.	**No cuelgue.**	noh KWAYL-gay

Buy a handy phone card *(tarjeta telefónica)* at a tobacco shop. Insert the card into a phone and call anywhere in the world. See "Let's Talk Telephones" near the end of this book for tips on making calls.

Finding a Room

If you keep it very simple and use these phrases, you will be able to reserve a hotel room over the phone. A good time to reserve a room is the morning of the day you plan to arrive. Related words and phrases can be found in the Telephone and Time sections.

Key Spanish room-finding words:

hotel	**hotel**	oh-TEHL
small, family-run hotel	**pensión**	payn-see-OHN
government-run inn	**parador**	pah-rah-DOR
room in private home	**habitación**	ah-bee-tah-thee-OHN
youth hostel	**albergue de juventud**	ahl-BEHR-gay day hoo-behn-TOOD
room	**habitación**	ah-bee-tah-thee-OHN
people	**personas**	pehr-SOH-nahs
night	**noche**	NOH-chay
arrive	**llegar**	yay-GAR
today	**hoy**	oy
tomorrow	**mañana**	mahn-YAH-nah
vacancy sign (literally "rooms," "beds")	**habitaciones, camas**	ah-bee-tah-thee-OH-nays, KAH-mahs

Handy Spanish hotel-hunting phrases:

I'd like to reserve a room...	**Quería reservar una habitación...**	keh-REE-ah ray-sehr-BAR OO-nah ah-bee-tah-thee-OHN
Do you have a room for...?	**¿Tiene una habitación libre para...?**	tee-EHN-ay OO-nah ah-bee-tah-thee-OHN LEE-bray PAH-rah
...one person / two people	**...una persona / dos personas**	OO-nah pehr-SOH-nah/ dohs pehr-SOH-nahs
...tonight	**...hoy**	oy
...two nights	**...dos noches**	dohs NOH-chays
...this Monday night	**...la noche de este lunes**	lah NOH-chay day AYS-tay LOO-nays
...Monday, August 28	**...el lunes, 28 de agosto**	ehl LOO-nays bayn-tay-OH-choh day ah-GOH-stoh
with / without / and	**con / sin / y**	kohn / seen / ee
...toilet	**...aseo**	ah-SAY-oh
...shower	**...ducha**	DOO-chah
...private bathroom	**...baño privado**	BAHN-yoh pree-VAH-doh
...double bed	**...cama de matrimonio**	KAH-mah day mah-tree-MOH-nee-oh
...twin beds	**...camas gemelas**	KAH-mahs hay-MAY-lahs
...view	**...vista**	BEE-stah

with only a sink	**solo con lavabo**	SOH-loh kohn lah-BAH-boh
How much does it cost?	**¿Cuánto cuesta?**	KWAHN-toh KWAYS-tah

You may hear: *"Lo siento"* (I'm sorry). *"El hotel está completo"* (The hotel is full). Or, *"Tiene que llegar antes de las quatro de la tarde"* (You must arrive before 4:00 p.m.).

To prompt an easy-to-understand answer, ask a question, and then say, *"¿Sí o no?"* (Yes or no?)

Spanish hotels come with a handy government-regulated classification system. Look for a blue and white plaque by the hotel door indicating the category and price range:

Hotel (H): The most comfortable and expensive.

Hostal-Residencia (HsR): Basically a hotel without a restaurant -- not to be confused with youth "hostals."

Pensión (P), Casa de Huéspedes (CH), and **Fonda (F):** Cheaper, usually family-run places. If you're on a tight budget, these can be a good value.

Parador: Government-run hotels, often in refurbished castles or palaces. They can be a good value, but most feature snooty staffs and rooms costing well over $100 per double.

Working out the details:

My name is...	**Mi nombre es...**	mee NOHM-bray ays
I'm coming now.	**Voy ahora.**	boy ah-OH-rah
I'll arrive in one hour.	**Voy a llegar dentro de una hora.**	boy ah yay-GAR DEHN-troh day OO-nah OH-rah
I'll arrive before 4:00 p.m.	**Voy a llegar antes de las cuatro de la tarde.**	boy ah yay-GAR AHN-tays day lahs KWAH-troh day lah TAR-day
We arrive Monday, depart Wednesday.	**Llegamos el lunes, salimos el miércoles.**	yay-GAH-mohs ehl LOO-nays, sah-LEE-mohs ehl mee-EHR-koh-lays
I have a reservation.	**Tengo la reserva hecha.**	TAYN-goh lah ray-SEHR-bah AY-chah
Confirm my reservation.	**Confirme mi reserva.**	kohn-FEER-may mee ray-SEHR-bah
I'll sleep anywhere.	**Puedo dormir en cualquier sitio.**	PWAY-doh DOR-meer ayn kwahl-kee-EHR SEE-tee-oh
I have a sleeping bag.	**Tengo un saco de dormir.**	TAYN-goh oon SAH-koh day dor-MEER
How much is your cheapest room?	**¿Cuánto cuesta su habitación más barata?**	KWAHN-toh KWAYS-tah soo ah-bee-tah-thee-OHN mahs bah-RAH-tah

Is it cheaper if I stay three nights?	¿Es más barato si quedo tres noches?	ays mahs bah-RAH-toh see KAY-doh trays NOH-chays
I will stay three nights.	Me quedaré tres noches.	may kay-dah-RAY trays NOH-chays
Is breakfast included?	¿El desayuno está incluido?	ehl day-sah-YOO-noh ays-TAH een-kloo-EE-doh
How much without breakfast?	¿Cuánto cuesta sin el desayuno?	KWAHN-toh KWAYS-tah seen ehl day-sah-YOO-noh
Complete price?	¿El precio completo?	ehl PRAY-thee-oh kohm-PLAY-toh
Service included?	¿Está el servicio incluido?	ays-TAH ehl sehr-BEE-thee-oh een-kloo-EE-doh
Can I see the room?	¿Puedo ver la habitación?	PWAY-doh behr lah ah-bee-tah-thee-OHN
Show me another room.	Enséñeme otra habitación.	ayn-SAYN-yay-may OH-trah ah-bee-tah-thee-OHN
Do you have something...?	¿Tiene algo...?	tee-EHN-ay AHL-goh
...larger / smaller	...más grande / más pequeño	mahs GRAHN-day / mahs pay-KAYN-yoh
...better / cheaper	...mejor / más barato	may-HOR / mahs bah-RAH-toh
...in the back	...en la parte de atrás	ayn lah PAR-tay day ah-TRAHS

...quieter	**...más silencioso**	mahs see-lehn-thee-OH-soh
No, thank you.	**No, gracias.**	noh GRAH-thee-ahs
Very good.	**Muy bien.**	MOO-ee bee-YEHN
I'll take it.	**La quiero.**	lah kee-EHR-oh
My key, please.	**Mi llave, por favor.**	mee YAH-bay por fah-BOR
Sleep well.	**Que duerma bien.**	kay DWEHR-mah bee-YEHN
Good night.	**Buenas noches.**	BWAY-nahs NOH-chays

Spanish hotel help and hassles:

I'd like...	**Quería...**	keh-REE-ah
...clean sheets.	**...unas sábanas limpias.**	OO-nahs SAH-bah-nahs LEEM-pee-ahs
...a pillow.	**...una almohada.**	OO-nah ahl-moh-AH-dah
...a blanket.	**...una manta.**	OO-nah MAHN-tah
...a towel.	**...una toalla.**	OO-nah toh-AH-yah
...toilet paper.	**...papel higiénico.**	pah-PEHL ee-hee-AY-nee-koh
...a crib.	**...una cuna.**	OO-nah KOO-nah
...an extra roll-away bed.	**...una cama plegable extra.**	OO-nah KAH-mah play-GAH-blay AYK-strah
...silence.	**...silencio.**	see-LEHN-thee-oh
Is there an elevator?	**¿Hay un ascensor?**	ī oon ahs-thehn-SOR

Come with me.	**Venga conmigo.**	VAYN-gah kohn-MEE-goh
I have a problem in my room.	**Tengo un problema en mi habitación.**	TAYN-goh oon proh-BLAY-mah ayn mee ah-bee-tah-thee-OHN
bad odor	**mal olor**	mahl oh-LOR
bugs	**moscas**	MOH-skahs
cockroaches	**cucarachas**	koo-kah-RAH-chahs
mice	**ratones**	rah-TOH-nays
prostitutes	**prostitutas**	proh-stee-TOO-tahs
The bed is too soft / hard.	**La cama es muy blanda / dura.**	lah KAH-mah ays MOO-ee BLAHN-dah / DOO-rah
I'm covered with bug bites.	**Estoy lleno de picaduras de mosquitos.**	ays-TOY YAY-noh day pee-kah-DOO-rahs day moh-SKEE-tohs
There is no hot water.	**No hay agua caliente.**	noh ī AH-gwah kahl-YEHN-tay
When is the water hot?	**¿Cuándo hay agua caliente?**	KWAHN-doh ī AH-gwah kahl-YEHN-tay
Where can I... my laundry?	**¿Dónde puedo... mi ropa?**	DOHN-day PWAY-doh... mee ROH-pah
...wash	**...lavar**	lah-BAR
...hang	**...tender**	tehn-DEHR
I'd like to stay another night.	**Quería quedarme otra noche.**	keh-REE-ah kay-DAR-may OH-trah NOH-chay

Where shall I park?	**¿Dónde voy a aparcar?**	DOHN-day boy ah ah-par-KAR
What time do you lock up?	**¿A qué hora cierran la puerta?**	ah kay OH-rah thee-AY-rahn lah PWEHR-tah
What time is breakfast?	**¿A qué hora es el desayuno?**	ah kay OH-rah ays ehl day-sah-YOO-noh
Wake me at 7:00.	**Despiérteme a las 7:00.**	days-pee-EHR-tay-may ah lahs see-EH-tay

If the management treats you like a *cucaracha*, ask to see the hotel's *libro de reclamaciones* (the government-required complaint book). Your problems will generally get solved in a jiffy.

Checking out in Spain:

I'l leave... / We'll leave...	**Me iré... / Nos iremos...**	may ee-RAY / nohs ee-RAY-mohs
...today / tomorrow.	**...hoy / mañana.**	oy / mahn-YAH-nah
When is check-out time?	**¿Cuándo es la hora de salida?**	KWAHN-doh ays lah OH-rah day sah-LEE-dah
Can I pay now?	**¿Le pago ahora?**	lay PAH-goh ah-OH-rah
The bill, please.	**La cuenta, por favor.**	lah KWAYN-tah por fah-BOR
Do you accept credit cards?	**¿Acepta tarjetas de crédito?**	ahk-THEHP-tah tar-*HAY*-tahs day KRAY-dee-toh

I slept like a log. (Sleep grabbed me.)	**Dormí de un tirón.**	dor-MEE day oon tee-ROHN
Everything was great.	**Todo estuvo muy bien.**	TOH-doh ays-TOO-boh MOO-ee bee-YEHN
Can I leave my bag here...?	**¿Me pueden guardar aquí la maleta...?**	may PWAY-dehn gwar-DAR ah-KEE lah mah-LAY-tah
Can we leave our bags here...?	**¿Podemos guardar aquí las maletas...?**	poh-DAY-mohs gwar-DAR ah-KEE lahs mah-LAY-tahs
...until ___	**...hasta ___**	AH-stah

Spanish camping:

tent	**tienda de campaña**	tee-EHN-dah day kahm-PAHN-yah
camping	**camping**	KAHM-peeng
The nearest campground?	**¿El camping más cercano?**	ehl KAHM-peeng mahs thehr-KAH-noh
Can I / Can we...?	**¿Puedo / Podemos...?**	PWAY-doh / poh-DAY-mohs
...camp here for one night	**...acampar aquí por una noche**	ah-kahm-PAR ah-KEE por OO-nah NOH-chay
Do showers cost extra?	**¿Cuestan extra las duchas?**	KWAYS-tahn AYK-strah lahs DOO-chahs

Eating

Finding a restaurant in Spain:

Where's a good... restaurant?	¿Dónde hay un buen restaurante...?	DOHN-day ī oon bwayn rays-toh-RAHN-tay
...cheap	...barato	bah-RAH-toh
...local-style	...regional	ray-hee-oh-NAHL
...untouristy	...que no sea un sitio de turistas	kay noh SAY-ah oon SEE-tee-oh day too-REES-tahs
...Chinese	...chino	CHEE-noh
...fast food	...comida rápida	koh-MEE-dah RAH-pee-dah

Ordering meals in Spanish:

What would you like?	¿Qué va a tomar?	kay bah ah toh-MAR
I'd like...	Quería...	keh-REE-ah
...a table for two.	...una mesa para dos.	OO-nah MAY-sah PAH-rah dohs
...non-smoking.	...no fumadores.	noh foo-mah-DOH-rays
...just a drink.	...solo para una bebida.	SOH-loh PAH-rah OO-nah bay-BEE-dah
...a snack.	...un pincho.	oon PEEN-choh
...to see the menu.	...ver el menú.	behr ehl may-NOO

...to order a meal.	**...ordenar la comida.**	or-day-NAR lah koh-MEE-dah
...to eat.	**...comer.**	koh-MEHR
...to pay.	**...pagar.**	pah-GAR
...to throw up.	**...vomitar.**	boh-mee-TAR
What do you recommend?	**¿Qué es lo que me recomienda?**	kay ays loh kay may ray-koh-mee-EHN-dah
What's your favorite?	**¿Cuál es su preferida?**	kwahl ays soo pray-fay-REE-dah
Is it...?	**¿Es esto...?**	ays AYS-toh
...good	**...sabroso**	sah-BROH-soh
...expensive	**...caro**	KAH-roh
...light	**...ligero**	lee-*HAY*-roh
Is it filling?	**¿Esto te llena?**	AYS-toh tay YAY-nah
What is...?	**¿Qué es...?**	kay ays
...that	**...esto**	AYS-toh
...local	**...típico**	TEE-pee-koh
...fast	**...lo más rápido**	loh mahs RAH-pee-doh
...cheap and filling	**...lo que llena y es barato**	loh kay YAY-nah ee ays bah-RAH-toh
Do you have...?	**¿Tiene...?**	tee-EHN-ay
...an English menu	**...un menú en inglés**	oon may-NOO ayn een-GLAYS
...children's portions	**...raciónes para niños**	rah-thee-OH-nays PAH-rah NEEN-yohs

The Spanish eat very late, and so should you if you'll be eating in restaurants. No self-respecting restaurant serves dinner before around 8 p.m. To eat early, well, and within even the tightest budget, duck into a bar, where you can stab toothpicks into local munchies (see *tapas* on page 60).

Dietary restrictions:

I'm allergic to...	**Soy alérgico[a] a...**	soy ah-LEHR-hee-koh ah
I cannot eat...	**No puedo comer...**	noh PWAY-doh koh-MEHR
...dairy products.	**...productos lácteos.**	proh-DOOK-tohs LAHK-tay-ohs
...fat.	**...grasa.**	GRAH-sah
...meat.	**...carne.**	KAR-nay
...salt.	**...sal.**	sahl
...sugar.	**...azúcar.**	ah-THOO-kar
I am diabetic.	**Soy diabético[a].**	soy dee-ah-BAY-tee-koh
No alcohol.	**No alcohol.**	noh ahl-KOHL
I am a...	**Soy...**	soy
...vegetarian.	**...vegetariano[a].**	bay-hay-tah-ree-AH-noh
...strict vegetarian.	**...estricto[a] vegetariano[a].**	ays-TREEK-toh bay-hay-tah-ree-AH-noh
...carnivore.	**...carnívoro[a].**	kar-NEE-boh-roh

Key Spanish menu words:

breakfast	**desayuno**	day-sah-YOO-noh
lunch	**almuerzo**	ahl-MWEHR-thoh
dinner	**cena**	THAY-nah
menu of the day	**menú del día**	may-NOO dayl DEE-ah
combination plate	**plato combinado**	PLAH-toh kohm-bee-NAH-doh
special of the day	**especial del día**	ays-pay-thee-AHL dayl DEE-ah
specialty of the house	**especialidad de la casa**	ays-pay-thee-ah-lee-DAHD day lah KAH-sah
tourist menu	**menú de turista**	meh-NOO day too-REES-tah
appetizers	**aperitivos**	ah-pay-ree-TEE-bohs
salad	**ensalada**	ayn-sah-LAH-dah
bread	**pan**	pahn
soup	**sopa**	SOH-pah
first course	**primer plato**	pree-MEHR PLAH-toh
main course	**segundo plato**	say-GOON-doh PLAH-toh
meat	**carne**	KAR-nay
poultry	**aves**	AH-bays
seafood	**marisco**	mah-REE-skoh
egg dishes	**tortillas**	tor-TEE-yahs
side dishes	**a parte**	ah PAR-tay

vegetables	**verduras**	behr-DOO-rahs
cheese	**queso**	KAY-soh
dessert	**postres**	POH-strays
beverages	**bebidas**	bay-BEE-dahs
beer	**cerveza**	thehr-BAY-thah
wine	**vino**	BEE-noh
service included	**servicio incluido**	sehr-BEE-thee-oh een-kloo-EE-doh
service not included	**servicio no incluido**	sehr-BEE-thee-oh noh een-kloo-EE-doh
with / and / or / without	**con / y /** **o / sin**	kohn / ee / oh / seen

Restaurant requests and regrets:

A little.	**Un poco.**	oon POH-koh
More.	**Más.**	mahs
Another.	**Otro.**	OH-troh
I did not order this.	**No ordené esto.**	noh or-day-NAY AYS-toh
Is this included with the meal?	**¿Está esto incluido** **con la comida?**	ays-TAH AYS-toh een-kloo-EE-doh kohn lah koh-MEE-dah
What time does this open / close?	**¿A qué hora** **abren / cierran?**	ah kay OH-rah AH- brehn / thee-AY-rahn
I'm in a hurry.	**Estoy en un apuro.**	ays-TOY ayn oon ah-POO-roh

I have an appointment at...	**Tengo una cita en...**	TAYN-goh OO-nah THEE-tah ayn
When will the food be ready?	**¿Cuando estará la comida lista?**	KWAHN-doh ays-tah-RAH lah koh-MEE-dah LEES-tah
I've changed my mind.	**Cambié de idea.**	kahm-bee-AY day ee-DAY-ah
Can I get it "to go"?	**¿Me lo empaqueta para llevar?**	may loh aym-pah-KAY-tah PAH-rah yay-BAR
This is...	**Esto es...**	AYS-toh ays
...dirty.	**...sucio.**	SOO-thee-oh
...greasy.	**...grasiento.**	grah-see-EHN-toh
...salty.	**...salado.**	sah-LAH-doh
...undercooked.	**...crudo.**	KROO-doh
...overcooked.	**...muy hecho.**	MOO-ee AY-choh
...inedible.	**...incomible.**	een-koh-MEE-blay
...cold.	**...frío.**	FREE-oh
Can you heat this up?	**¿Me puede calentar esto?**	may PWAY-day kah-lehn-TAR AYS-toh
Yuk!	**¡Que asco!**	kay AHS-koh
Do your customers return?	**¿Sus clientes vuelven?**	soos klee-EHN-tays BWEHL-behn
Enough.	**Suficiente.**	soo-fee-thee-EHN-tay
Finished.	**Terminado.**	tehr-mee-NAH-doh
Delicious!	**¡Delicioso!**	day-lee-thee-OH-soh
I'm wonderfully stuffed!	**¡Me he puesto las botas!**	may ay PWAYS-toh lahs BOH-tahs

Paying for your meal:

Waiter.	**Camarero.**	kah-mah-RAY-roh
Waitress.	**Camarera.**	kah-mah-RAY-rah
The bill, please.	**La cuenta, por favor.**	lah KWAYN-tah por fah-BOR
Together.	**Junto.**	*H*OON-toh
Separate checks.	**En cheques separados.**	ayn CHAY-kays say-pah-RAH-dohs
Do you accept credit cards?	**¿Acepta tarjetas de crédito?**	ahk-THEHP-tah tar-*H*AY-tahs day KRAY-dee-toh
Is there a cover charge?	**¿Hay un precio de entrada?**	ī oon PRAY-thee-oh day ayn-TRAH-dah
Is service included?	**¿Está el servicio incluido?**	ays-TAH ehl sehr-BEE-thee-oh een-kloo-EE-doh
This is not correct.	**Esto no es correcto.**	AYS-toh noh ays koh-REHK-toh
Can you explain this?	**¿Me puede explicar esto?**	may PWAY-day ayk-splee-KAR AYS-toh
What if I wash the dishes?	**¿Qué le parece si lavo los platos?**	kay lay pah-RAY-thay see LAH-boh lohs PLAH-tohs
Keep the change.	**Quédese con el cambio.**	KAY-day-say kohn ehl KAHM-bee-oh
This is for you.	**Esto es para usted.**	AYS-toh ays PAH-rah oos-TEHD

On a Spanish table:

table	**mesa**	MAY-sah
plate	**plato**	PLAH-toh
napkin	**servilleta**	sehr-vee-YAY-tah
knife	**cuchillo**	koo-CHEE-yoh
fork	**tenedor**	tay-nay-DOR
spoon	**cuchara**	koo-CHAH-rah
glass	**vaso**	BAH-soh
carafe	**garrafa**	gah-RAH-fah
water	**agua**	AH-gwah

Spanish edible extras:

bread	**pan**	pahn
butter	**mantequilla**	mahn-tay-KEE-yah
margarine	**margarina**	mar-gah-REE-nah
salt	**sal**	sahl
pepper	**pimienta**	pee-mee-EHN-tah
sugar	**azúcar**	ah-THOO-kar
artifical sweetener	**edulcorante**	ay-dool-koh-RAHN-tay
honey	**miel**	mee-EHL
mustard	**mostaza**	mohs-TAH-thah
mayonnaise	**mayonesa**	mah-yoh-NAY-sah
olives	**aceitunas**	ah-thay-TOO-nahs
pickles	**pepinillos**	pay-pee-NEE-yohs
garlic	**ajo**	AH-hoh

What's for breakfast:

breakfast	**desayuno**	day-sah-YOO-noh
eggs	**huevos**	WAY-bohs
fried eggs	**huevos fritos**	WAY-bohs FREE-tohs
scrambled eggs	**huevos revueltos**	WAY-bohs ray-BWEHL-tohs
boiled egg...	**huevo cocido...**	WAY-boh koh-THEE-doh
...soft	**...pasado por agua**	pah-SAH-doh por AH-gwah
...hard	**...duro**	DOO-roh
omelet	**tortilla**	tor-TEE-yah
potato omelet	**tortilla española**	tor-TEE-yah ays-pahn-YOH-lah
ham	**jamón**	hah-MOHN
cheese	**queso**	KAY-soh
bread	**pan**	pahn
roll	**panecillo**	pah-nay-THEE-yoh
toast	**tostadas**	tohs-TAH-dahs
jelly	**gelatina**	hay-lah-TEE-nah
pastry	**pasteles**	pahs-TAY-lays
fritters	**churros**	CHOO-rohs
yogurt	**yogur**	yoh-GOOR
cereal	**cereales**	thay-ray-AH-lays
milk	**leche**	LAY-chay

hot cocoa	**chocolate caliente**	choh-koh-LAH-tay kahl-YEHN-tay
fruit juice	**zumo de fruta**	THOO-moh day FROO-tah
orange juice	**zumo de naranja**	THOO-moh day nah-RAHN-hah
coffee / tea (see Drinking)	**café / té**	kah-FAY / tay
Is breakfast included (in the room cost)?	**¿El desayuno está incluido?**	ehl day-sah-YOO-noh ays-TAH een-kloo-EE-doh

The traditional Spanish breakfast is *churros con chocolate* -- greasy, cigar-shaped fritters or doughnuts dipped in pudding-like chocolate. Try these at least once. For a more solid breakfast I prefer a slice of *tortilla española,* the hearty potato omelet that most cafés serve every morning. Add a little bread and *café con leche,* and you've got a cheap, filling meal.

Spanish tapas:

aceitunas rellenas	stuffed olives
albóndigas	spiced meatballs with sauce
almejas a la marinera	clams in paprika sauce
atún	tuna
calamares fritos	fried squid
callos	chickpeas with tripe and sauce

caña	glass of draft beer
chorizo al vino	Spanish sausage cooked in wine
empanadillas	pastries stuffed with meat or seafood
gambas	prawns
gambas a la plancha	grilled prawns
garbanzos	marinated chickpeas
jamón serrano	smoked ham
judías verdes	green beans
pinchos de queso	pieces of cheese
pan	bread
pescaditos fritos	assorted fried fish
pinchos morunos	skewer of pork flavored with paprika
salmón ahumado	smoked salmon
tortilla	omelet (usually made with potatoes)

Bars called *tascas* or *tabernas* offer delicious appetizers called *tapas* during "normal" American-style eating hours when Spanish restaurants are still closed. If you want to eat a cheap, quick, tasty meal before the sun sets, do the "Tapa Tango." Just point to the food you want and say, *"un pincho"* for a bite-sized serving, *"una tapa"* for a larger serving, *"una ración"* for a generous serving, or *"un bocadillo"* for an appetizer sandwich.

Spanish soups and salads:

soup	**sopa**	SOH-pah
broth...	**caldo...**	KAHL-doh
...chicken	**...pollo**	POH-yoh
...meat	**...carne**	KAR-nay
...fish	**...de pescado**	day pay-SKAH-doh
...with noodles	**...con tallarines**	kohn tah-yah-REE-nays
...with rice	**...con arroz**	kohn ah-ROHTH
seafood soup	**sopa de mariscos**	SOH-pah day mah-REES-kohs
chilled soup	**gazpacho**	gahth-PAH-choh
thick vegetable soup	**puré de vegetales**	poo-RAY day bay-*hay*-TAH-lays
green salad	**ensalada verde**	ayn-sah-LAH-dah BEHR-day
chef's salad	**ensalada de la casa**	ayn-sah-LAH-dah day lah KAH-sah
lettuce	**lechuga**	lay-CHOO-gah
tomatoes	**tomates**	toh-MAH-tays
cucumbers	**pepinos**	pay-PEE-nohs
oil / vinegar (typical dressing)	**aceite / vinagre**	ah-THAY-tay / bee-NAH-gray
What is in this salad?	**¿Que tiene esta ensalada?**	kay tee-EHN-ay AYS-tah ayn-sah-LAH-dah

Try *gazpacho*, a chilled soup made with tomatoes, cucumbers, onions, and bell peppers.

Spanish seafood:

seafood	**marisco**	mah-REE-skoh
assorted sea-food	**marisco variado**	mah-REE-skoh bah-ree-AH-doh
fish	**pescado**	pay-SKAH-doh
cod	**bacalao**	bah-kahl-OW
salmon	**salmón**	sahl-MOHN
trout	**trucha**	TROO-chah
tuna	**atún**	ah-TOON
herring	**arenque**	ah-RAYN-kay
sardines	**sardinas**	sar-DEE-nahs
anchovies	**anchoas**	ahn-CHOH-ahs
clams	**almejas**	ahl-MAY-*h*ahs
mussels	**mejillones**	may-*hee*-YOH-nays
oysters	**ostras**	OH-strahs
prawns	**gambas**	GAHM-bahs
large prawns	**langostinos**	lahn-goh-STEE-nohs
crab	**cangrejo**	kahn-GREH-*h*oh
lobster	**langosta**	lahn-GOH-stah
octopus	**pulpo**	POOL-poh
squid	**calamares**	kah-lah-MAH-rays
Where did this live?	**¿Dónde vivía este?**	DOHN-day bee-BEE-ah AYS-tay

Spanish poultry and meat:

poultry	**aves**	AH-bays
chicken	**pollo**	POH-yoh
turkey	**pavo**	PAH-boh
duck	**pato**	PAH-toh
meat	**carne**	KAR-nay
beef	**carne de vaca**	KAR-nay day BAH-kah
roast beef	**carne asada**	KAR-nay ah-SAH-dah
beef steak	**biftec**	BEEF-tayk
ribsteak	**riñones**	reen-YOH-nays
veal	**ternera**	tehr-NAY-rah
cutlet	**chuleta**	choo-LAY-tah
pork	**cerdo**	THEHR-doh
ham	**jamón**	hah-MOHN
lamb	**cabrito**	kah-BREE-toh
bunny	**conejo**	koh-NAY-hoh
brains	**sesos**	SAY-sohs
tongue	**lengua**	LEHN-gwah
liver	**hígado**	EE-gah-doh
tripe	**tripa**	TREE-pah
horse	**caballo**	kah-BAH-yoh
How long has this been dead?	**¿Cuánto tiempo hace que lo mataron?**	KWAHN-toh tee-EHM-poh AH-thay kay loh mah-tah-ROHN

How it's prepared in Spain:

hot	**caliente**	kahl-YEHN-tay
cold	**frío**	FREE-oh
raw	**crudo**	KROO-doh
cooked	**cocinado**	koh-thee-NAH-doh
baked	**asado**	ah-SAH-doh
boiled	**cocido**	koh-THEE-doh
fillet	**filete**	fee-LAY-tay
fresh	**fresco**	FRAY-skoh
fried	**frito**	FREE-toh
grilled	**a la plancha**	ah lah PLAHN-chah
microwave	**microondas**	mee-kroh-OHN-dahs
mild	**templado**	tehm-PLAH-doh
poached	**escalfado**	ays-kahl-FAH-doh
roasted	**asado**	ah-SAH-doh
smoked	**ahumado**	ah-oo-MAH-doh
spicy hot	**picante**	pee-KAHN-tay
steamed	**hervido**	ehr-BEE-doh
stuffed	**rellenos**	ray-YAY-nohs
rare	**poco hecho**	POH-koh AY-choh
medium	**medio**	MAY-dee-oh
well-done	**muy hecho**	MOO-ee AY-choh

Spanish veggies, pasta and rice:

vegetables	**verduras**	behr-DOO-rahs
artichoke	**alcachofa**	ahl-kah-CHOH-fah
asparagus	**espárragos**	ays-PAH-rah-gohs
beans	**judías**	*h*oo-DEE-ahs
beets	**remolacha**	ray-moh-LAH-chah
broccoli	**brécol**	BRAY-kohl
cabbage	**repollo**	ray-POH-yoh
carrots	**zanahorias**	thah-nah-OH-ree-ahs
cauliflower	**coliflor**	koh-lee-FLOR
corn	**maíz**	mah-EETH
eggplant	**berenjena**	bay-rehn-*H*AY-nah
green beans	**judías verdes**	*h*oo-DEE-ahs BEHR-days
green peppers	**pimientos verdes**	pee-mee-EHN-tohs BEHR-days
mushrooms	**setas**	SAY-tahs
onions	**cebollas**	thay-BOH-yahs
peas	**guisantes**	gee-SAHN-tays
spinach	**espinacas**	ay-spee-NAH-kahs
zucchini	**calabacín**	kah-lah-bah-THEEN
potato	**patata**	pah-TAH-tah
French fries	**patatas fritas**	pah-TAH-tahs FREE-tahs
pasta	**pasta**	PAH-stah
spaghetti	**espaguetis**	ays-pah-GEH-tees
rice	**arroz**	ah-ROHTH

Spanish specialties to watch for:

cochinillo asado	roasted suckling pig marinated in herbs, oil and white wine (Segovia & Toledo)
empanada gallega	a pizza-like pie of beef, pork or seafood combined with onions, tomatoes, and bell peppers
fabada asturiana	beans, pork and paprika stew
horchata	refreshing almond-flavored drink served at outdoor food and drink stalls
paella	saffron-flavored rice with seafood and sausage
pimientos a la riojana	sweet peppers stuffed with minced meat
pisto	vegetarian stew of zucchini, tomatoes, and bell peppers
riñones al jerez	kidneys in a sherry sauce

Nuts to you:

almond	**almendra**	ahl-MAYN-drah
chestnut	**castaña**	kah-STAHN-yah
hazelnut	**avellana**	ah-bay-YAH-nah
peanut	**cacahuete**	kah-kah-WAY-tay
pistachio	**pistacho**	pee-STAH-choh
walnut	**nuez**	noo-ayth

Spanish fruit:

fruit	**fruta**	FROO-tah
apple	**manzana**	mahn-THAH-nah
apricot	**albaricoque**	ahl-bah-ree-KOH-kay
banana	**plátano**	PLAH-tah-noh
cherry	**cereza**	thay-RAY-thah
coconut	**coco**	KOH-koh
date	**dátile**	DAH-tee-lay
fig	**higo**	EE-goh
grapefruit	**pomelo**	poh-MAY-loh
grapes	**uvas**	OO-bahs
lemon	**limón**	lee-MOHN
melon	**melón**	may-LOHN
orange	**naranja**	nah-RAHN-*h*ah
peach	**melocotón**	may-loh-koh-TOHN
pear	**pera**	PAY-rah
pineapple	**piña**	PEEN-yah
plum	**ciruela**	theer-WAY-lah
prune	**ciruela seca**	theer-WAY-lah SAY-kah
raspberry	**frambuesa**	frahm-BWAY-sah
strawberry	**fresa**	FRAY-sah
tangerine	**mandarina**	mahn-dah-REE-nah
watermelon	**sandía**	sahn-DEE-ah

Spanish desserts and goodies:

dessert	**postres**	POH-strays
flan	**flan**	flahn
cake	**bizcocho**	beeth-KOH-choh
ice cream cake	**tarta helada**	TAR-tah ay-LAH-dah
ice cream	**helado**	ay-LAH-doh
sherbet	**sorbete**	sor-BAY-tay
fruit cup	**variado de fruta**	bah-ree-AH-doh day FROO-tah
tart	**tarta**	TAR-tah
whipped cream	**nata montada**	NAH-tah mohn-TAH-dah
mousse	**mousse**	moos
pudding	**pudín**	poo-DEEN
pastry	**pasteles**	pahs-TAY-lays
cookies	**galletas, pastas**	gah-YAY-tahs, PAH-stahs
candy	**caramelo**	kah-rah-MAY-loh
low calorie	**bajo en calorías**	BAH-hoh ayn kah-loh-REE-ahs
homemade	**hecho en casa**	AY-choh ayn KAH-sah
Superb!	**¡Riquísimo!**	ree-KEE-see-moh
Exquisite!	**¡Exquisito!**	ayk-see-SEE-toh

While you're in Salamanca, Toledo, or Madrid, snack on a bag of *Obleas.* It's like eating sweet communion wafers the size of paper plates.

Drinking

Spanish water, milk, and juice:

mineral water	**agua mineral**	AH-gwah mee-nay-RAHL
tap water	**agua del grifo**	AH-gwah dayl GREE-foh
whole milk	**leche**	LAY-chay
skim milk	**leche desnatada**	LAY-chay days-nah-TAH-dah
fresh milk	**leche fresca**	LAY-chay FRAY-skah
hot chocolate	**chocolate caliente**	choh-koh-LAH-tay kahl-YEHN-tay
fruit juice (pure)	**zumo de fruta (puro)**	THOO-moh day FROO-tah (POO-roh)
orange juice	**zumo de naranja**	THOO-moh day nah-RAHN-hah
with / without...	**con / sin...**	kohn / seen
...carbonation	**...burbujas**	boor-BOO-hahs
...sugar	**...azúcar**	ah-THOO-kar
...ice	**...hielo**	YAY-loh
glass / cup	**vaso / taza**	BAH-soh / TAH-thah
small / large	**pequeña / grande**	pay-KAYN-yah / GRAHN-day
bottle	**botella**	boh-TAY-yah
Is the water safe to drink?	**¿Es el agua potable?**	ays ehl AH-gwah poh-TAH-blay

Spanish coffee and tea:

coffee...	**café...**	kah-FEH
...espresso	**...espreso**	ays-PREH-soh
...black	**...solo**	SOH-loh
...with a little milk	**...cortado**	kor-TAH-doh
...with a lot of milk	**...con leche**	kohn LAY-chay
...with sugar	**...con azúcar**	kohn ah-THOO-kar
...American-syle	**...americano**	ah-may-ree-KAH-noh
...decaffeinated	**...descafeinado**	days-kah-fay-NAH-doh
...instant	**...soluble**	soh-LOO-blay
hot water	**agua caliente**	AH-gwah kahl-YEHN-tay
tea / lemon	**té / limón**	tay / lee-MOHN
tea bag	**infusion de té**	een-foo-see-OHN day tay
iced tea	**té con hielo**	tay kohn YAY-loh
small / large	**corto / largo**	KOR-toh / LAR-goh
Another cup.	**Otra taza.**	OH-trah TAH-thah

When ordering coffee at a bar, you'll notice that the menu board lists three price levels: prices are cheapest in the *barra* (bar), higher at the *mesa* (table), and highest on the *terraza* (terrace).

Spanish wine:

wine	**vino**	BEE-noh
table wine	**vino de mesa**	BEE-noh day MAY-sah
cheap house wine	**vino de la casa**	BEE-noh day lah KAH-sah
local	**local**	loh-KAHL
red	**tinto**	TEEN-toh
white	**blanco**	BLAHN-koh
rose	**rosado**	roh-SAH-doh
sparkling	**espumoso**	ays-poo-MOH-soh
sweet	**dulce**	DOOL-thay
medium	**semi-seco**	say-mee-SAY-koh
dry	**seco**	SAY-koh
very dry	**muy seco**	MOO-ee SAY-koh
A glass...	**Un vaso...**	oon BAH-soh
A carafe...	**Una garrafa...**	OO-nah gah-RAH-fah
A bottle...	**Una botella...**	OO-nah boh-TAY-yah
...of red wine.	**...de vino tinto.**	day BEE-noh TEEN-toh
...of white wine.	**...de vino blanco.**	day BEE-noh BLAHN-koh
The wine list.	**La lista de vinos.**	lah LEE-stah day BEE-nohs

A carafe of house wine with your meal is often very cheap in Spanish restaurants.

Spanish beer:

beer	**cerveza**	thehr-BAY-thah
glass of draft beer	**caña**	KAHN-yah
big glass of draft beer	**tubo**	TOO-boh
bottle	**botella**	boh-TAY-yah
small / large	**pequeña / grande**	pay-KAYN-yah / GRAHN-day
light / dark	**rubia / negra**	ROO-bee-ah / NAY-grah
local / imported	**local / importada**	loh-KAHL / eem-por-TAH-dah
alcohol-free	**sin-alcohol**	seen-ahl-KOHL
cold	**fría**	FREE-ah
colder	**más fría**	mahs FREE-ah

Spanish bar talk:

What would you like?	**¿Qué quiere?**	kay kee-AY-ray
local specialty	**especialidad regional**	ays-pay-thee-ah-lee-DAHD ray-hee-oh-NAHL
straight	**solo**	SOH-loh
with / without...	**con / sin...**	kohn / seen
...alcohol	**...alcohol**	ahl-KOHL
...ice	**...hielo**	YAY-loh
One more.	**Otro.**	OH-troh

Cheers!	**¡Salud!**	sahl-LOOD
Let's make a toast to...!	**¡Vamos a brindar por...!**	BAH-mohs ah breen-DAR por
...you	**...usted**	oos-TEHD
...Spain	**...España**	ays-PAHN-yah
I'm feeling...	**Me siento...**	may see-EHN-toh
...a little drunk.	**...un poco borracho[a].**	oon POH-koh boh-RAH-choh
...blitzed.	**...borracho[a].**	boh-RAH-choh

Groceries and Picnics

Spanish picnic words:

open air market	**mercado municipal**	mehr-KAH-doh moo-nee-thee-PAHL
supermarket	**supermercado**	soo-pehr-mehr-KAH-doh
picnic	**picnic**	peek-NEEK
sandwich	**bocadillo**	boh-kah-DEE-yoh
roll	**panecillo**	pah-nay-THEE-yoh
bread	**pan**	pahn
whole wheat bread	**pan de trigo**	pahn day TREE-goh
ham	**jamón**	*h*ah-MOHN
smoked ham	**jamón serrano**	*h*ah-MOHN say-RAH-noh
sausage	**salchichón**	sahl-chee-CHOHN
cheese	**queso**	KAY-soh
mild / sharp	**suave / fuerte**	SWAH-bay / FWEHR-tay
yogurt	**yogur**	yoh-GOOR
plastic spoon	**cuchara de plástico**	koo-CHAH-rah day PLAHS-tee-koh
plastic cup	**vaso de plástico**	BAH-soh day PLAHS-tee-koh
paper plate	**plato de papel**	PLAH-toh day PAH-pehl

At the Spanish grocery:

Is it self-service?	**¿Es auto-servicio?**	ays OW-toh-sehr-BEE-thee-oh
May I taste a little?	**¿Podría probarlo?**	poh-DREE-ah proh-BAR-loh
Fifty grams.	**Cincuenta gramos.**	theen-KWEHN-tah GRAH-mohs
One hundred grams.	**Cien gramos.**	thee-EHN GRAH-mohs
More. / Less.	**Más. / Menos.**	mahs / MAY-nohs
A piece.	**Un trozo.**	oon TROH-thoh
A slice.	**Una rodaja.**	OO-nah roh-DAH-hah
Sliced.	**En rodajas.**	ayn roh-DAH-hahs
Will you make me a sandwich?	**¿Me puede hacer un bocadillo?**	may PWAY-day ah-THEHR oon boh-kah-DEE-yoh
To take out.	**Para llevar.**	PAH-rah yay-BAR
Is there a park nearby?	**¿Hay un parque cerca de aquí?**	ī oon PAR-kay THEHR-kah day ah-KEE
May we picnic here?	**¿Podemos picnic aquí?**	poh-DAY-mohs peek-NEEK ah-KEE
Enjoy your meal!	**¡Qué aproveche!**	kay ah-proh-VAY-chay

While you can opt for the one-stop *supermercado* (supermarket), it's more fun to assemble your picnic and practice your Spanish visiting the various small shops. One hundred grams is about ¼ pound.

Sightseeing

Handy Spanish sightseeing questions:

Where is / are...?	¿Dónde está / están...?	DOHN-day ays-TAH / ays-TAHN
...the best view	...la mejor vista	lah may-HOR BEE-stah
...the main square	...la plaza principal	lah PLAH-thah preen-thee-PAHL
...the old town center	...el casco viejo	ehl KAHS-koh bee-AY-hoh
...the city hall	...el ayuntamiento	ehl ī-oon-tah-mee-EHN-toh
...the museum	...el museo	ehl moo-SAY-oh
...the castle	...el castillo	ehl kahs-TEE-yoh
...the palace	...el palacio	ehl pah-LAH-thee-oh
...the ruins	...las ruinas	lahs RWEE-nahs
...a festival	...un festival	oon fays-tee-VAHL
...a fair	...una feria	OO-nah feh-REE-ah
...the tourist information office	...la Oficina de Turismo	lah oh-fee-THEE-nah day too-REES-moh
Do you have... in English?	¿Tiene... en inglés?	tee-EHN-ay... ayn een-GLAYS
...information	...información	een-for-mah-thee-OHN
...a guidebook	...una guía	OO-nah GEE-ah
...a tour	...una visita	OO-nah bee-SEE-tah

When is the next tour...?	¿Cuándo es la siguiente visita...?	KWAHN-doh ays lah seeg-ee-EHN-tay bee-SEE-tah
...in English	...en inglés	ayn een-GLAYS
Is it free?	¿Es esto gratis?	ays AYS-toh grah-TEES
How much does it cost?	¿Cuánto cuesta?	KWAHN-toh KWAYS-tah
Is there a discount for...?	¿Tienen descuento para...?	tee-EH-nehn days-KWEHN-toh PAH-rah
...youth	...la juventud	lah *hoo*-behn-TOOD
...students	...estudiantes	ays-too-dee-AHN-tays
...seniors	...la tercera edad	lah tehr-THAY-rah ay-DAHD
Is the ticket good all day?	¿Es válido el billete para todo el día?	ays BAH-lee-doh ehl bee-YEH-tay PAH-rah TOH-doh ehl DEE-ah
What time does this open / close?	¿A qué hora abren / cierran?	ah kay OH-rah AH-brehn / thee-AY-rahn
What time is the last entry?	¿A qué hora es la última entrada?	ah kay OH-rah ays lah OOL-tee-mah ayn-TRAH-dah
PLEASE let me in.	Por favor, déjeme entrar.	por fah-BOR DAY-*hay*-may ayn-TRAR
I've traveled all the way from...	He viajado desde...	ay bee-ah-*HAH*-doh DEHS-day
I must leave tomorrow.	Tengo que irme mañana.	TAYN-goh kay EER-may mahn-YAH-nah

In the museum:

Where can I find this? (point to photo)	¿Dónde puedo encontrar esto?	DOHN-day PWAY-doh ayn-kohn-TRAR AYS-toh
I'd like to see...	Quería ver...	keh-REE-ah behr
Can I...?	¿Puedo...?	PWAY-doh
...take photos	...sacar fotos	sah-KAR FOH-tohs
...use a video camera	...usar la grabadora de vídeo	oo-SAR lah grah-bah-DOH-rah day BEE-day-oh
No flash / tripod.	No flash / trípode.	noh flahsh / TREE-poh-day
I like it.	Me gusta.	may GOO-stah
It's so...	Es tan...	ays tahn
...beautiful.	...bonito.	boh-NEE-toh
...ugly.	...feo.	FAY-oh
...strange.	...extraño.	ayk-STRAHN-yoh
...boring.	...aburrido.	ah-boo-REE-doh
...interesting.	...interesante.	een-tay-ray-SAHN-tay
Wow!	¡Caray!	kah-RĪ
My feet hurt!	¡Me duelen los pies!	may DWAY-lehn lohs pee-AYS
I'm exhausted!	¡Estoy cansadísimo[a]!	ays-TOY kahn-sah-DEE-see-moh

Art and architecture:

art	**arte**	AR-tay
artist	**artista**	ar-TEES-tah
painting	**cuadro**	KWAH-droh
self portrait	**autorretrato**	ow-toh-ray-TRAH-toh
sculptor	**escultor**	ays-kool-TOR
sculpture	**escultura**	ays-kool-TOO-rah
architect	**arquitecto**	ar-kee-TEHK-toh
architecture	**arquitectura**	ar-kee-tehk-TOO-rah
original	**original**	oh-ree-*hee*-NAHL
restored	**restaurado**	rays-tow-RAH-doh
B.C.	**A.C.**	AHN-tays day KREE-stoh
A.D.	**D.C.**	days-PWAYS day KREE-stoh
century	**siglo**	SEE-gloh
style	**estilo**	ays-TEE-loh
Abstract	**Abstracto**	ahb-STRAHK-toh
Ancient	**Antiguo**	ahn-TEE-gwoh
Art Nouveau	**Modernista**	moh-dehr-NEES-tah
Baroque	**Barroco**	bah-ROH-koh
Classical	**Clásico**	KLAH-see-koh
Gothic	**Gótico**	GOH-tee-koh
Impressionist	**Impresionismo**	eem-pray-see-oh-NEES-moh
Medieval	**Medieval**	may-dee-ah-VAHL

Moorish	**Moros**	MOH-rohs
Renaissance	**Renacimiento**	ray-nah-thee-mee-EHN-toh
Romanesque	**Románico**	roh-MAH-nee-koh
Romantic	**Romanticismo**	roh-mahn-tee-THEES-moh

Art terms unique to Spain:

Alcazaba	A Moorish castle
Alcazar	A Moorish castle or palace
Azulejo	Blue tiles
Churrigueresque	Super-thick Spanish Baroque, named after a local artist
Moriscos	The Islamic Arabs (Moors) who ruled much of Spain and Portugal from 711 to 1492
Mozarabs	Christians in Spain under Moorish rule
Mudejar	The Gothic-Islamic style of the Moors in Spain after the Christian conquest
Plateresque	The frilly late Gothic of Spain

The Moorish culture left a deep mark on Iberia. An understanding of the Moorish occupation will help you better understand your sightseeing.

Castles and palaces:

castle	**castillo**	kah-STEE-yoh
palace	**palacio**	pah-LAH-thee-oh
ballroom	**salón de baile**	sah-LOHN day BĪ-lay
kitchen	**cocina**	koh-THEE-nah
cellar	**bodega**	boh-DAY-gah
dungeon	**calabozo**	kah-lah-BOH-thoh
fortified walls	**paredes fortificadas**	pah-RAY-days for-tee-fee-KAH-dahs
tower	**torre**	TOR-ray
fountain	**fuente**	FWEHN-tay
garden	**jardín**	har-DEEN
king	**rey**	ray
queen	**reina**	ray-EE-nah
knights	**caballería**	kah-bah-yay-REE-ah

Spanish religious words:

cathedral	**catedral**	kah-tay-DRAHL
church	**iglesia**	ee-GLAY-see-ah
monastery	**monasterio**	moh-nahs-TAY-ree-oh
mosque	**mezquita**	mayth-KEE-tah
synagogue	**sinagoga**	see-nah-GOH-gah
chapel	**capilla**	kah-PEE-yah
altar	**altar**	ahl-TAR
altarpiece	**tesoro**	tay-SOH-roh

cross	**cruz**	krooth
sacristy	**sacristia**	sah-krees-TEE-ah
crypt	**cripta**	KREEP-tah
dome	**cúpula**	KOO-poo-lah
organ	**órgano**	OR-gah-noh
choir	**coro**	KOH-roh
relic	**reliquia**	ray-LEE-kee-ah
saint	**santo[a]**	SAHN-toh
God	**Dios**	DEE-ohs
Jewish	**judío**	*hoo*-DEE-oh
Muslim	**musulmán**	moo-sool-MAHN
Christian	**cristiano**	kree-stee-AH-noh
Protestant	**protestante**	proh-tays-TAHN-tay
Catholic	**católico**	kah-TOH-lee-koh
When is the mass / service?	**¿A qué hora es la misa / servicio?**	ah kay OH-rah ays lah MEE-sah / sehr-BEE-thee-oh
Are there concerts in the church?	**¿Hay conciertos en la iglesia?**	ī kohn-thee-EHR-tohs ayn lah ee-GLAY-see-ah

Shopping

Names of Spanish shops:

antiques	**anticuarios**	ahn-tee-KWAH-ree-ohs
art gallery	**galería de arte**	gah-lay-REE-ah day AR-tay
bakery	**panadería**	pah-nah-deh-REE-ah
barber shop	**barbería**	bar-beh-REE-ah
beauty parlor	**peluquería**	pay-loo-keh-REE-ah
book shop	**librería**	lee-bray-REE-ah
camera shop	**tienda de fotos**	tee-EHN-dah day FOH-tohs
department store	**grandes almacenes**	GRAHN-days ahl-mah-THAY-nays
flea market	**rastro**	RAHS-troh
flower market	**floristería**	floh-rees-teh-REE-ah
grocery store	**supermercado**	soo-pehr-mehr-KAH-doh
jewelry shop	**joyería**	hoy-eh-REE-ah
laundromat	**lavandería**	lah-bahn-deh-REE-ah
newsstand	**kiosco**	kee-OH-skoh
open air market	**mercado municipal**	mehr-KAH-doh moo-nee-thee-PAHL
pharmacy	**farmacia**	far-MAH-thee-ah
shopping mall	**centro comercial**	THEHN-troh koh-mehr-thee-AHL

souvenir shop	**tienda de souvenirs**	tee-EHN-dah day soo-bay-NEERS
supermarket	**supermercado**	soo-pehr-mehr-KAH-doh
toy store	**tienda de juguetes**	tee-EHN-dah day *hoo*-GAY-tays
travel agency	**agencia de viajes**	ah-*HAYN*-thee-ah day bee-AH-*hays*
used bookstore	**tienda de libros usados**	tee-EHN-dah day LEE-brohs oo-SAH-dohs
wine shop	**tienda de vinos**	tee-EHN-dah day BEE-nohs

In Spain, shops are closed for a long lunch from 13:30 until about 16:30, and all day on Sundays. Local souvenirs and postcards are cheapest in the big department stores. *El Corte Inglés* is Spain's ultimate department store, providing everything from cheap souvenirs to train and theater tickets to haircuts on Sundays. Madrid's is a block uphill from the *Puerta del Sol*.

If you brake for garage sales, you'll pull a U-turn for Madrid's *El Rastro* flea market. Europe's best flea market sprawls for miles each Sunday.

You can look up words for different colors and fabrics in the *Rolling Rosetta Stone* Word Guide near the end of this book.

Shop till you drop:

sale	**rebajas**	ray-BAH-hahs
How much does it cost?	**¿Cuánto cuesta?**	KWAHN-toh KWAYS-tah
I'd like...	**Quería...**	keh-REE-ah
Do you have...?	**¿Tiene usted...?**	tee-EHN-ay oos-TEHD
...something cheaper	**...algo más barato**	AHL-goh mahs bah-RAH-toh
...more	**...más**	mahs
Can I see...?	**¿Puedo ver...?**	PWAY-doh behr
This one.	**Este.**	AYS-tay
Can I try it on?	**¿Puedo probarlo?**	PWAY-doh proh-BAR-loh
Do you have a mirror?	**¿Tiene un espejo?**	tee-EHN-ay oon ays-PAY-hoh
It's too...	**Es muy...**	ays MOO-ee
...big.	**...grande.**	GRAHN-day
...small.	**...pequeño.**	pay-KAYN-yoh
...expensive.	**...caro.**	KAH-roh
Did you make this?	**¿Hizo usted esto?**	EE-thoh oos-TEHD AYS-toh
What is this made of?	**¿De qué está hecho esto?**	day kay ays-TAH AY-choh AYS-toh
Is it machine washable?	**¿Se puede lavar en la lavadora?**	say PWAY-day lah-BAR ayn lah lah-bah-DOH-rah
Will it shrink?	**¿Esto encoge?**	AYS-toh ayn-KOH-hay

Can you ship this?	¿Puede enviar esto?	PWAY-day ayn-bee-AR AYS-toh
Do you accept credit cards?	¿Acepta tarjetas de crédito?	ahk-THEHP-tah tar-HAY-tahs day KRAY-dee-toh
Tax-free?	¿Libre de impuestos?	LEE-bray day eem-PWAYS-tohs
I'll think about it.	Voy a pensármelo.	boy ah payn-SAR-may-loh
What time do you close?	¿A qué hora cierran?	ah kay OH-rah thee-AY-rahn
What time do you open tomorrow?	¿A qué hora abren mañana?	ah kay OH-rah AH-brehn mahn-YAH-nah
Is that your best price?	¿Es éste su mejor precio?	ays AYS-tay soo may-HOR PRAY-thee-oh
My last offer.	Mi ùltima oferta.	mee OOL-tee-mah oh-FEHR-tah
I'm nearly broke.	Casi no tengo dinero.	KAH-see noh TAYN-goh dee-NAY-roh
I'm... / We're...	Estoy... / Estamos...	ays-TOY / ays-TAH-mohs
...browsing.	...mirando.	mee-RAHN-doh
My friend...	Mi amigo[a]...	mee ah-MEE-goh
My husband...	Mi marido...	mee mah-REE-doh
My wife...	Mi mujer...	mee moo-HEHR
...has the money.	...tiene el dinero.	tee-EHN-ay ehl dee-NAY-roh

Mail

Licking the Spanish postal code:

post office	**oficina de correos**	oh-fee-THEE-nah day koh-RAY-ohs
stamp	**sello**	SAY-yoh
post card	**postal**	poh-STAHL
letter	**carta**	KAR-tah
aerogram	**aerograma**	ī-roh-GRAH-mah
envelope	**sobre**	SOH-bray
package	**paquete**	pay-KAY-tay
box	**caja**	KAH-hah
string	**cordón**	kor-DOHN
tape	**cinta adhesiva**	THEEN-tah ah-day-SEE-bah
mailbox	**buzón**	boo-THOHN
air mail	**por avión**	por ah-bee-OHN
express	**rápido**	RAH-pee-doh
surface mail (slow and cheap)	**por barco**	por BAR-koh
book rate	**tarifa**	tah-REE-fah
registered	**certificada**	thehr-tee-fee-KAH-dah
insured	**asegurada**	ah-say-goo-RAH-dah
fragile	**frágil**	FRAH-heel
contents	**contenido**	kohn-teh-NEE-doh

customs	**aduana**	ah-DWAH-nah
to / from	**a / desde**	ah / DEHS-day
address	**dirección**	dee-rehk-thee-OHN
zip code	**código postal**	KOH-dee-goh poh-STAHL
general delivery (poste restante)	**Lista de Correos**	LEE-stah day koh-RAY-ohs

Mail bonding:

Where is the post office?	**¿Dónde está la oficina de correos?**	DOHN-day ays-TAH lah oh-fee-THEE-nah day koh-RAY-ohs
Which window for...?	**¿Cuál es la ventana para...?**	kwahl ays lah bayn-TAH-nah PAH-rah
To the United States.	**Para los Estados Unidos.**	PAH-rah lohs ays-TAH-dohs oo-NEE-dohs
How much does it cost?	**¿Cuánto cuesta?**	KWAHN-toh KWAYS-tah
How many days...?	**¿Cuántos días...?**	KWAHN-tohs DEE-ahs
How many weeks...?	**¿Cuántas semanas...?**	KWAHN-tahs say-MAH-nahs
How many months...?	**¿Cuántos meses...?**	KWAHN-tohs MAY-says
...will it take	**...tardará**	tar-dah-RAH

In Spain, you can often get stamps at the corner *estanco* (tobacco shop). As long as you know which stamps you need, this is a great convenience.

Time

Spanish time:

What time is it?	¿Qué hora es?	kay OH-rah ays
It's...	Son las...	sohn lahs
...8:00 in the morning.	...ocho de la mañana.	OH-choh day lah mahn-YAH-nah
...16:00.	...dieciséis.	dee-ay-thee-SAYS
...9:30 in the evening.	...nueve y media de la noche.	NWAY-bay ee MAY-dee-ah day lah NOH-chay
...a quarter past three.	...las tres y cuarto.	lahs trays ee KWAR-toh
...a quarter to eleven.	...las once menos cuarto.	lahs OHN-thay MAY-nohs KWAR-toh
...about 4:00 in the afternoon.	...sobre las 4:00 de la tarde.	SOH-bray lahs KWAH-troh day lah TAR-day
...noon.	...doce.	DOH-thay
...midnight.	...doce de la noche.	DOH-thay day lah NOH-chay
...too early.	...demasiado temprano.	day-mah-see-AH-doh tehm-PRAH-noh
...too late.	...demasiado tarde.	day-mah-see-AH-doh TAR-day

Timely words:

minute	**minuto**	mee-NOO-toh
hour	**hora**	OH-rah
in one hour	**dentro de una hora**	DEHN-troh day OO-nah OH-rah
immediately	**inmediatamente**	een-may-dee-ah-tah-MEHN-tay
any time	**a cualquier hora**	ah kwahl-kee-EHR OH-rah
every hour	**cada hora**	KAH-dah OH-rah
every day	**cada día**	KAH-dah DEE-ah
May 15	**15 de mayo**	KEEN-thay day MAH-yoh
in the morning	**por la mañana**	por lah mahn-YAH-nah
in the afternoon	**por la tarde**	por lah TAR-day
in the evening	**por la noche**	por lah NOH-chay
night	**noche**	NOH-chay
day	**día**	DEE-ah
today	**hoy**	oy
yesterday	**ayer**	ah-YEHR
tomorrow	**mañana**	mahn-YAH-nah
tomorrow morning	**mañana por la mañana**	mahn-YAH-nah por lah mahn-YAH-nah

week	**semana**	say-MAH-nah
month	**mes**	mays
year	**año**	AHN-yoh
last	**último**	OOL-tee-moh
this	**este**	AYS-tay
next	**próximo**	PROHK-see-moh
Monday	**lunes**	LOO-nays
Tuesday	**martes**	MAR-tays
Wednesday	**miércoles**	mee-EHR-koh-lays
Thursday	**jueves**	*H*WAY-bays
Friday	**viernes**	bee-EHR-nays
Saturday	**sábado**	SAH-bah-doh
Sunday	**domingo**	doh-MEEN-goh
January	**enero**	ay-NAY-roh
February	**febrero**	fay-BRAY-roh
March	**marzo**	MAR-thoh
April	**abril**	AH-breel
May	**mayo**	MAH-yoh
June	**junio**	*H*OON-yoh
July	**julio**	*H*OOL-yoh
August	**agosto**	ah-GOH-stoh
September	**septiembre**	sehp-tee-EHM-bray
October	**octubre**	ohk-TOO-bray
November	**noviembre**	noh-bee-EHM-bray
December	**diciembre**	dee-thee-EHM-bray

spring	**primavera**	pree-mah-BAY-rah
summer	**verano**	bay-RAH-noh
fall	**otoño**	oh-TOHN-yoh
winter	**invierno**	een-bee-EHR-noh
Ice Age	**Edad de Hielo**	ay-DAHD day YAY-loh

Happy holidays:

holiday	**festivo**	fay-STEE-boh
national holiday	**festivo nacional**	fay-STEE-boh nah-thee-oh-NAHL
religious holiday	**día religioso**	DEE-ah ray-lee-hee-OH-soh
Happy birthday!	**¡Feliz cumpleaños!**	fay-LEETH koom-play-AHN-yohs
Happy anniversary!	**¡Feliz aniversario!**	fay-LEETH ah-nee-behr-SAH-ree-oh
Merry Christmas!	**¡Feliz Navidad!**	fay-LEETH nah-vee-DAHD
Happy New Year!	**¡Feliz Año Nuevo!**	fay-LEETH AHN-yoh NWAY-boh

Semana Santa (Holy Week), which leads up to Easter, is a festive time throughout Iberia, especially in Sevilla. The bulls run through Pamplona (and some people) every July. Other holidays include *Corpus Christi* (in early June), *Ascensión de Maria* (August 15th), and *Dia de la Hispanidad* (Spain's national holiday, October 12th).

Red Tape and Profanity

Filling out Spanish forms:

Sr. / Sra. / Srta.	Mr. / Mrs. / Miss
nombre	first name
apellido	last name
dirección	address
domicilio	address
calle	street
ciudad	city
estado	state
país	country
nacionalidad	nationality
origen / destino	origin / destination
edad	age
fecha de nacimiento	date of birth
lugar de nacimiento	place of birth
sexo	sex
masculino	male
femenino	female
casado / casada	married man / married woman
soltero / soltera	single man / single woman
profesión	profession
adulto	adult
niño / niña	boy / girl
niños	children
familia	family
firma	signature
fecha	date

Spanish profanity:

Go to hell!	**¡Vete al infierno!**	BAY-tay ahl een-fee-EHR-noh
Kiss my ass.	**Bésame culo.**	BAY-sah-may KOO-loh
bastard	**bastardo**	bahs-TAR-doh
bitch	**perra**	PEHR-rah
child of a whore	**hijo[a] de puta**	EE-*h*oh day POO-tah
breasts (colloq.)	**tetas**	TAY-tahs
penis (colloq.)	**polla, minga**	POH-yah, MEEN-gah
shit	**mierda**	mee-EHR-dah
drunk	**borracho[a]**	boh-RAH-choh
idiot	**idiota**	ee-dee-OH-tah
imbecile	**imbécil**	eem-BAY-theel
jerk (horned sheep)	**cabrón[a]**	kah-BROHN
stupid	**estúpido[a]**	ays-TOO-pee-doh
Did someone...?	**¿Hizo alguien...?**	EE-thoh AHL-gee-ehn
...fart	**...un pedo**	oon PAY-doh
...burp	**...un erupto**	oon ay-ROOP-toh

Like most Mediterranean people, the Spanish employ some colorful gestures. For a run-down on these, see Gestures near the end of this book.

Health

Handy Spanish health words:

pain	**dolor**	doh-LOR
dentist	**dentista**	dayn-TEES-tah
doctor	**doctor[a]**	dohk-TOR
nurse	**enfermera**	ayn-fehr-MAY-rah
health insurance	**seguro médico**	say-GOO-roh MAY-dee-koh
hospital	**hospital**	oh-spee-TAHL
medicine	**medicina**	may-dee-THEE-nah
pharmacy	**farmacia**	far-MAH-thee-ah
prescription	**receta**	ray-THAY-tah
pill	**píldora**	PEEL-doh-rah
aspirin	**aspirina**	ah-spee-REE-nah
antibiotic	**antibiótico**	ahn-tee-bee-OH-tee-koh
pain killer	**analgésico**	ah-nahl-*HAY*-see-koh
bandage	**venda**	BAYN-dah

Finding a cure:

I feel sick.	**Estoy enfermo[a].**	ays-TOY ayn-FEHR-moh
I need a doctor...	**Necesito un doctor...**	nay-thay-SEE-toh oon dohk-TOR
...who speaks English.	**...que hable inglés.**	kay AH-blay een-GLAYS
It hurts here.	**Me duele aquí.**	may DWAY-lay ah-KEE
I'm allergic to...	**Soy alérgico[a] a...**	soy ah-LEHR-*hee*-koh ah
...penicillin.	**...penicilina.**	pay-nee-thee-LEE-nah
I am diabetic.	**Soy diabético[a].**	soy dee-ah-BAY-tee-koh
This is serious.	**Esto es serio.**	AYS-toh ays SAY-ree-oh
I have...	**Tengo...**	TAYN-goh
...a burn.	**...una quemadura.**	OO-nah kay-mah-DOO-rah
...chest pains.	**...dolor de pecho.**	doh-LOR day PAY-choh
...a cold.	**...un resfriado.**	oon rays-free-AH-doh
...constipation.	**...estreñimiento.**	ays-trayn-yee-mee-EHN-toh
...a cough.	**...catarro.**	kah-TAH-roh
...diarrhea.	**...diarrea.**	dee-ah-RAY-ah
...a fever.	**...fiebre.**	fee-AY-bray
...the flu.	**...gripe.**	GREE-pay

...the giggles.	**...la risa en la boca.**	lah REE-sah ayn lah BOH-kah
...a headache.	**...dolor de cabeza.**	doh-LOR day kah-BAY-thah
...indigestion.	**...indigestión.**	een-dee-*h*ays-tee-OHN
...an infection.	**...una infección.**	OO-nah een-fehk-thee-OHN
...nausea.	**...náuseas.**	NOW-see-ahs
...a rash.	**...erupción.**	ay-roop-thee-OHN
...a sore throat.	**...dolor de garganta.**	doh-LOR day gar-GAHN-tah
...a stomach ache.	**...dolor de estómago.**	doh-LOR day ays-TOH-mah-goh
...a swelling.	**...un hinchazón.**	oon een-chah-THOHN
...a toothache.	**...dolor de muelas.**	doh-LOR day moo-AY-lahs
...a venereal disease.	**...una enfermedad venérea.**	OO-nah ayn-fehr-may-DAHD vay-NAY-ray-ah
...worms.	**...lombrices.**	lohm-BREE-thays
I have body odor.	**Huelo a sudor.**	WAY-loh ah soo-DOR
Is it serious?	**¿Es esto serio?**	ays AYS-toh SAY-ree-oh

Help!

Help in general:

Help!	**¡Ayuda!**	ah-YOO-dah
Help me!	**!Ayúdenme!**	ah-YOO-dehn-may
Call a doctor!	**¡Llamen a un médico!**	YAH-mehn ah oon MAY-dee-koh
ambulance	**ambulancia**	ahm-boo-LAHN-thee-ah
accident	**accidente**	ahk-thee-DEHN-tay
injured	**herido**	ay-REE-doh
emergency	**emergencia**	ay-mehr-HAYN-thee-ah
fire	**fuego**	FWAY-goh
police	**policía**	poh-lee-THEE-ah
thief	**ladrón**	lah-DROHN
pick-pocket	**carterista**	kar-tay-REES-tah
I've been ripped off.	**Me han robado.**	may ahn roh-BAH-doh
I've lost...	**He perdido...**	ay pehr-DEE-doh
...my passport.	**...mi pasaporte.**	mee pah-sah-POR-tay
...my ticket.	**...mi billete.**	mee bee-YEH-tay
...my baggage.	**...mis maletas.**	mees mah-LAY-tahs
...my purse.	**...mi bolso.**	mee BOHL-soh
...my wallet.	**...mi cartera.**	mee kar-TAY-rah
...my faith in humankind.	**...mi fe en los seres humanos.**	mee fay ayn lohs SAY-rays oo-MAH-nohs
I'm lost.	**Estoy perdido[a].**	ays-TOY pehr-DEE-doh

Help for women:

Leave me alone.	**Déjame sola.**	DAY-hah-may SOH-lah
I wish to be alone.	**Me gustaría estar sola.**	may goo-stah-REE-ah ays-TAR SOH-lah
I'm not interested.	**No estoy interesada.**	noh ays-TOY een-tay-ray-SAH-dah
I'm married.	**Estoy casada.**	ays-TOY kah-SAH-dah
I'm a lesbian.	**Soy lesbiana.**	soy lehs-bee-AH-nah
I have a contagious disease.	**Tengo una enfermedad contagiosa.**	TAYN-goh OO-nah ayn-fehr-may-DAHD kohn-tah-hee-OH-sah
Stop following me.	**No me siga.**	noh may SEE-gah
Don't touch me.	**No me toque.**	noh may TOH-kay
Enough!	**¡Basta!**	BAH-stah
Get lost!	**¡Vete!**	BAY-tay
Drop dead!	**¡Vete al infierno!**	BAY-tay ahl een-fee-EHR-noh
I'll call the police!	**¡Voy a llamar a la policía!**	boy ah yah-MAR ah lah poh-lee-THEE-ah
Police!	**¡Policía!**	poh-lee-THEE-ah

Whenever macho males threaten to make girl-watching a contact sport, local women stroll holding hands or arm-in-arm. This means "we're not interested." Wearing conservative clothes and avoiding smiley eye contact also conveys a "don't hustle me" message.

Conversations

Getting to know you:

My name is...	**Me llamo...**	may YAH-moh
What's your name?	**¿Cómo se llama?**	KOH-moh say YAH-mah
How are you?	**¿Cómo está?**	KOH-moh ays-TAH
Very well, thanks.	**Muy bien, gracias.**	MOO-ee bee-YEHN GRAH-thee-ahs
I am... / You are...	**Estoy... / Está...**	ays-TOY / ays-TAH
...happy.	**...contento[a].**	kohn-TEHN-toh
...sad.	**...triste.**	TREE-stay
...tired.	**...cansado[a].**	kahn-SAH-doh
...thirsty.	**...sediento[a].**	say-dee-EHN-toh
I am... / You are...	**Tengo... / Tiene...**	TAYN-goh / tee-EHN-ay
...hungry.	**...hambre.**	AHM-bray
...lucky.	**...suerte.**	SWEHR-tay
...cold.	**...frío.**	FREE-oh
I don't smoke.	**No fumo.**	noh FOO-moh
Where are you from?	**¿De dónde es?**	day DOHN-day ays
What city?	**¿Qué ciudad?**	kay thee-oo-DAHD
What country?	**¿Qué país?**	kay pah-EES
What planet?	**¿Qué planeta?**	kay plah-NAY-tah
I am American.	**Soy americano[a].**	soy ah-may-ree-KAH-noh

I am Canadian.	**Soy canadiense.**	soy kah-nah-dee-EHN-say
(This is) my...	**Mi...**	mee
...male friend / female friend.	**...amigo / amiga.**	ah-MEE-goh / ah-MEE-gah
...boyfriend / girlfriend.	**...novio / novia.**	NOH-bee-oh / NOH-bee-ah
...husband / wife.	**...marido / esposa.**	mah-REE-doh / ays-POH-sah
...son / daughter.	**...hijo / hija.**	EE-*h*oh / EE-*h*ah
...brother / sister.	**...hermano / hermana.**	ehr-MAH-noh / ehr-MAH-nah
...father / mother.	**...padre / madre.**	PAH-dray / MAH-dray

Family, school and work:

Are you married? (asked of a man)	**¿Está casado?**	ays-TAH kah-SAH-doh
Are you married? (asked of a woman)	**¿Está casada?**	ays-TAH kah-SAH-dah
Do you have children?	**¿Tiene hijos?**	tee-EHN-ay EE-*h*ohs
Do you have photos?	**¿Tiene fotos?**	tee-EHN-ay FOH-tohs
How old is your child?	**¿Cuántos años tiene su hijo[a]?**	KWAHN-tohs AHN-yohs tee-EHN-ay soo EE-*h*oh
Beautiful child!	**¡Qué niño[a] más guapo[a]!**	kay NEEN-yoh mahs GWAH-poh

Beautiful children!	¡Qué niños[as] más guapos[as]!	kay NEEN-yohs mahs GWAH-pohs
What are you studying?	¿Qué está estudiando?	kay ays-TAH ays-too-dee-AHN-doh
How old are you?	¿Cuántos años tiene?	KWAHN-tohs AHN-yohs tee-EHN-ay
I'm... years old.	Tengo... años.	TAYN-goh... AHN-yohs
Do you have brothers and sisters?	¿Tiene hermanos y hermanas?	tee-EHN-ay ehr-MAH-nohs ee ehr-MAH-nahs
What is your occupation?	¿En qué trabaja?	ayn kay trah-BAH-hah
I'm a...	Soy...	soy
...student.	...estudiante.	ays-too-dee-AHN-tay
...teacher.	...profesor[a].	proh-fay-SOR
...worker.	...trabajador[a].	trah-bah-hah-DOR
...brain surgeon.	...cirujano[a] de cerebro.	thee-roo-HAH-noh day say-RAY-broh
...professional traveler.	...viajante de profesión.	bee-ah-HAHN-tay day proh-fay-see-OHN
Do you like your work?	¿Le gusta su trabajo?	lay GOO-stah soo trah-BAH-hoh

Travel talk:

Are you on vacation?	¿Está de vacaciones?	ays-TAH day bah-kah-thee-OH-nays
A business trip?	¿Un viaje de negocios?	oon bee-AH-hay day nay-GOH-thee-ohs

How long have you been traveling?	¿Cuánto tiempo hace que están viajando?	KWAHN-toh tee-EHM-poh AH-thay kay ays-TAHN bee-ah-*HAHN*-doh
day / week	día / semana	DEE-ah / say-MAH-nah
month / year	mes / año	mays / AHN-yoh
When are you going home?	¿Cuándo va para casa?	KWAHN-doh bah PAH-rah KAH-sah
This is my first time in...	Esta es mi primera vez en...	AYS-tah ays mee pree-MAY-rah bayth ayn
I've visited... and then...	He visitado... y después...	ay bee-see-TAH-doh... ee days-PWAYS
Today / tomorrow I'll go to...	Hoy / mañana iré a...	oy / mahn-YAH-nah ee-RAY ah
I'm homesick.	Tengo morriña.	TAYN-goh moh-REEN-yah
I'm very happy here.	Estoy muy contento[a] aquí.	ays-TOY MOO-ee kohn-TEHN-toh ah-KEE
The Spanish are very friendly.	Los españoles son muy amables.	lohs ays-pahn-YOH-lays sohn MOO-ee ah-MAH-blays
Spain is a wonderful country.	España es un país precioso.	ays-PAHN-yah ays oon pah-EES pray-thee-OH-soh
To travel is to live.	Viajar es vivir.	bee-ah-*HAR* ays bee-BEER

Weather:

What will the weather be like tomorrow?	**¿Qué tiempo va a hacer mañana?**	kay tee-EHM-poh bah ah ah-THEHR mahn-YAH-nah
sunny / rainy	**asoleado / lluvioso**	ah-soh-lay-AH-doh / yoo-bee-OH-soh
hot / cold	**caluroso / frío**	kah-loo-ROH-soh / FREE-oh

Favorite things:

What's your favorite...?	**¿Cuál es su... favorito?**	kwahl ays soo... fah-voh-REE-toh
...art	**...arte**	AR-tay
...hobby	**...pasatiempo**	pah-sah-tee-EHM-poh
...ice cream	**...helado**	ay-LAH-doh
...male singer	**...cantante**	kahn-TAHN-tay
...male author	**...autor**	ow-TOR
...male movie star	**...actor**	ahk-TOR
...sport	**...deporte**	day-POR-tay
...vice	**...vicio**	BEE-thee-oh
What's your favorite...?	**¿Cuál es su... favorita?**	kwahl ays soo... fah-voh-REE-tah
...music	**...música**	MOO-see-kah
...female singer	**...cantante**	kahn-TAHN-tay
...female author	**...autora**	ow-TOH-rah
...female movie star	**...actriz**	ahk-TREETH
...movie	**...película**	pay-LEE-koo-lah

Responses for all occasions:

I like that.	**Eso me gusta.**	AY-soh may GOO-stah
I like you.	**Me cae bien.**	may kī bee-YEHN
That's great!	**¡Qué bien!**	kay bee-YEHN
Perfect.	**Perfecto.**	pehr-FEHK-toh
Funny.	**Divertido.**	dee-behr-TEE-doh
Very interesting.	**Muy interesante.**	MOO-ee een-tay-ray-SAHN-tay
Really?	**¿De verdad?**	day behr-DAHD
Wow!	**¡Caray!**	kah-RĪ
Congratulations!	**¡Felicidades!**	fay-lee-thee-DAH-days
You're welcome.	**De nada.**	day NAH-dah
Bless you! (after sneeze)	**¡Salud!**	sah-LOOD
What a pity!	**¡Qué lastima!**	kay lahs-TEE-mah
No problem.	**No hay problema.**	noh ī proh-BLAY-mah
O.K.	**De acuerdo.**	day ah-KWEHR-doh
That's life.	**Así es la vida.**	ah-SEE ays lah BEE-dah
This is the good life!	**¡Esto si que es vida!**	AYS-toh see kay ays BEE-dah
Have a good trip!	**¡Buen viaje!**	bwayn bee-AH-hay
Good luck!	**¡Buena suerte!**	BWAY-nah SWEHR-tay
Let's go!	**¡Vamos!**	BAH-mohs

Thanks a million:

You are...	**Usted es...**	oos-TEHD ays
...kind.	**...amable.**	ah-MAH-blay
...wonderful.	**...maravilloso[a].**	mah-rah-bee-YOH-soh
...generous.	**...generoso[a].**	*h*eh-nay-ROH-soh
You've been a tremendous help.	**Me ha ayudado mucho.**	may ah ī-yoo-DAH-doh MOO-choh
I will remember you...	**Le recordaré...**	lay ray-kor-dah-RAY
...always.	**...siempre.**	see-AYM-pray
...till Tuesday.	**...hasta el martes.**	AH-stah ehl MAR-tays

Conversing with Spanish animals:

rooster / cock-a-doodle-doo	**gallo / cacarea**	GAH-yoh / kah-kah-RAY-ah
bird / tweet tweet	**pajaro / pío pío**	pah-*H*AH-roh / PEE-oh PEE-oh
cat / meow	**gato / miau**	GAH-toh / MEE-ow
dog / woof woof	**perro / guao guao**	PEHR-roh / gwow gwow
duck / quack quack	**pato / cua cua**	PAH-toh / kwah kwah
cow / moo	**vaca / muh**	BAH-kah / moo
pig / oink oink	**cerdo / (just snort)**	THEHR-doh / (just snort)

Politics and Philosophy

The Spanish enjoy deep political conversations. With these lists, you can build sentences that will sound either deep or bizarre, depending on your mood (and theirs).

Political words relevant to Spain:

Basque ETA: Separatist Basque terrorist group.
Guerra Civil: The 1936-1939 Civil War, which ended with Franco's Nationalists (fascists aided by Hitler) overthrowing the Spanish Republican government (aided by the USSR and Hemingway).
Falange: Franco's fascist party.
Franco: Spain's fascist dictator from 1939 to 1975.
Gonzalez: Spain's current Socialist Prime Minister.
Guernica: Town destroyed by Franco during the Civil War, immortalized by a Picasso painting (now in Madrid).
Juan Carlos: Modern democratic king who succeeded Franco.
OTAN: NATO
Republicanos: Supporters of Spain's democratically elected government, overthrown by Franco's fascists.
Nacionalistas: Supporters of Franco during the Civil War.

Who:

politicians	**políticos**	poh-LEE-tee-kohs
big business	**gran negocio**	grahn nay-GOH-thee-oh
mafia	**mafia**	MAH-fee-ah
military	**militar**	mee-lee-TAR
fascists	**fascistas**	fahs-THEES-tahs
the system	**el sistema**	ehl sees-TAY-mah
the rich	**los ricos**	lohs REE-kohs
the poor	**los pobres**	lohs POH-brays
men / women	**hombres / mujeres**	OHM-brays / moo-*H*EH-rays
children	**niños**	NEEN-yohs
the Spanish	**los españoles**	lohs ays-pahn-YOH-lays
the Portuguese	**los portugueses**	lohs por-too-GAY-says
the French	**los franceses**	lohs frahn-THAY-says
the Germans	**los alemanes**	lohs ah-lay-MAH-nays
the Americans	**los americanos**	lohs ah-may-ree-KAH-nohs
I / you	**yo / usted**	yoh / oos-TEHD
everyone	**todo la gente**	TOH-doh lah *H*EHN-tay

What:

want	**querer**	keh-REHR
need	**necesitar**	nay-thay-see-TAR
take	**coger**	koh-*H*EHR
give	**dar**	dar
prosper	**prosperar**	proh-spay-RAR
suffer	**sufrir**	soof-REER
love	**amar**	ah-MAR
hate	**odiar**	oh-dee-AR
work	**trabajar**	trah-bah-*H*AR
play	**jugar**	*h*oo-GAR
vote	**votar**	boh-TAR

Why:

love	**amor**	ah-MOR
sex	**sexo**	SEHK-soh
money	**dinero**	dee-NAY-roh
power	**poder**	poh-DEHR
family	**familia**	fah-MEEL-yah
work	**trabajo**	trah-BAH-*h*oh
food	**comida**	koh-MEE-dah
health	**salud**	sah-LOOD
hope	**esperanza**	ays-pay-RAHN-thah
religion	**religión**	ray-lee-*h*ee-OHN
happiness	**alegría**	ah-lay-GREE-ah
recreational drugs	**drogas blandas**	DROH-gahs BLAHN-dahs
democracy	**democracia**	day-moh-krah-THEE-ah
taxes	**impuestos**	eem-PWAYS-tohs

lies	**mentiras**	mayn-TEE-rahs
corruption	**corrupción**	koh-roop-thee-OHN
racism	**racismo**	rah-THEES-moh
pollution	**polución**	poh-loo-thee-OHN
war / peace	**guerra / paz**	GEHR-rah / pahth

You be the judge:

(not) important	**(no es) importante**	(noh ays) eem-por-TAHN-tay
(not) powerful	**(no es) poderoso**	(noh ays) poh-day-ROH-soh
(not) honest	**(no es) honesto**	(noh ays) oh-NEHS-toh
(not) innocent	**(no es) inocente**	(noh ays) ee-noh-THEHN-tay
(not) greedy	**(no es) avaro**	(noh ays) ah-BAH-roh
liberal	**liberal**	lee-bay-RAHL
conservative	**conservativo**	kohn-sehr-bah-TEE-boh
radical	**radical**	rah-dee-KAHL
too much	**demasiado**	day-mah-see-AH-doh
enough	**suficiente**	soo-fee-thee-EHN-tay
never enough	**nunca suficiente**	NOON-kah soo-fee-thee-EHN-tay
same	**igual**	ee-GWAHL
better / worse	**mejor / peor**	may-HOR / pay-OR
good / bad	**bueno / malo**	BWAY-noh / MAH-loh
here	**aquí**	ah-KEE
everywhere	**en todas partes**	ayn TOH-dahs PAR-tays

Assorted beginnings and endings:

I (don't) like...	**(No) me gusta...**	(noh) may GOO-stah
Do you like...?	**¿Le gusta...?**	lay GOO-stah
I am... / Are you...?	**Yo soy... / ¿Es usted...?**	yoh soy / ays oos-TEHD
I (don't) believe...	**Yo (no) creo...**	yoh (noh) KRAY-oh
Do you believe...?	**¿Cree usted...?**	KRAY-yay oos-TEHD
...in God	**...en Dios**	ayn DEE-ohs
...in reincarnation	**...en la reencarnación**	ayn lah ray-ehn-kar-nah-thee-OHN
...in extraterrestrial life	**...en la vida extraterreste**	ayn lah BEE-dah ayk-strah-tay-REHS-tay
...in Clinton	**...en Clinton**	ayn "Clinton"
Yes. / No.	**Sí. / No.**	see / noh
Maybe. / I don't know.	**Tal vez. / No sé.**	tahl bayth / noh say
What's most important in life?	**¿Qué es lo más importante en la vida?**	kay ays loh mahs eem-por-TAHN-tay ayn lah BEE-dah
The problem is...	**El problema es...**	ehl proh-BLAY-mah ays
The answer is...	**La respuesta es...**	lah rehs-PWAYS-tah ays
We have solved the world's problems.	**Nosotros hemos resuelto los problemas del mundo.**	noh-SOH-trohs AY-mohs ray-SWAYL-toh lohs proh-BLAY-mahs dayl MOON-doh

Entertainment

What's happening:

movie...	**película...**	pay-LEE-koo-lah
...original version	**...versión original**	behr-see-OHN oh-ree-*hee*-NAHL
...in English	**...en inglés**	ayn een-GLAYS
...with subtitles	**...con subtítulos**	kohn soob-TEE-too-lohs
...dubbed	**...doblada**	doh-BLAH-dah
music...	**música...**	MOO-see-kah
...classical	**...clásica**	KLAH-see-kah
...folk	**...folklórica**	fohk-LOH-ree-kah
...live	**...en vivo**	ayn BEE-boh
rock	**rock**	rohk
jazz	**jazz**	"jazz"
blues	**blues**	"blues"
singer	**cantante**	kahn-TAHN-tay
concert	**concierto**	kohn-thee-EHR-toh
show	**espectáculo**	ays-pehk-TAH-koo-loh
dancing	**baile**	BĪ-lay
folk dancing	**baile folklórico**	BĪ-lay fohk-LOH-ree-koh
disco	**disco**	DEES-koh
cover charge	**entrada**	ayn-TRAH-dah

A night on the town:

Can you recommend...?	¿Me puede recomendar...?	may PWAY-day ray-koh-mehn-DAR
What's happening tonight?	¿Qué hay esta noche?	kay ī AYS-tah NOH-chay
Where can I buy a ticket?	¿Dónde puedo comprar un billete?	DOHN-day PWAY-doh kohm-PRAR oon bee-YEH-tay
When does it start?	¿Cuándo empieza esto?	KWAHN-doh aym-pee-AY-thah AYS-toh
When does it end?	¿Cuándo acaba esto?	KWAHN-doh ah-KAH-bah AYS-toh
Where's the best place to dance nearby?	¿Dónde está el más cercano y mejor sitio para bailar?	DOHN-day ays-TAH ehl mahs thehr-KAH-noh ee may-HOR SEE-tee-oh PAH-rah bī-LAR
Do you want to dance?	¿Quieres bailar conmigo?	kee-AY-rays bī-LAR kohn-MEE-goh
Again?	¿Otra más?	OH-trah mahs
It's been a wonderful night.	Ha sido una noche encantadora.	ah SEE-doh OO-nah NOH-chay ayn-kahn-tah-DOH-rah
Where is the best place to stroll?	¿Dónde está el mejor paseo?	DOHN-day ays-TAH ehl may-HOR pah-SAY-oh

For free, enjoyable entertainment, join the locals for a *paseo*, an evening stroll through town.

A Spanish Romance

Words of love:

I / me / you	**yo / mi / tu**	yoh / mee / too
flirt	**coquetear**	koh-kay-tay-AR
kiss	**besar**	bay-SAR
hug	**abrazar**	ah-brah-THAR
love	**amor**	ah-MOR
make love	**hacer el amor**	ah-THEHR ehl ah-MOR
condom	**condón**	kohn-DOHN
contraceptive	**contraceptivo**	kohn-trah-thehp-TEE-boh
safe sex	**sexo sin peligro**	SEHK-soh seen pay-LEE-groh
sexy	**sexy**	"sexy"
romantic	**romántico**	roh-MAHN-tee-koh
honey	**cariño[a]**	kah-REEN-yoh
my angel	**mi ángel**	mee AHN-hayl
my love	**mi amor**	mee ah-MOR
my heaven	**mi cielo**	mee thee-AY-loh

Ah, amor:

What's the matter?	**¿Qué le pasa?**	kay lay PAH-sah
Nothing.	**Nada.**	NAH-dah

I am...	**Soy...**	ays-TOY
...straight.	**...heterosexual.**	ay-tay-roh-sehk-soo-AHL
...gay.	**...homosexual.**	oh-moh-sehk-soo-AHL
...undecided.	**...indeciso[a].**	een-day-THEE-soh
...prudish.	**...prudente.**	proo-DEHN-tay
...horny.	**...caliente.**	kahl-YEHN-tay
We are on our honeymoon.	**Estamos de luna de miel.**	ays-TAH-mohs day LOO-nah day mee-EHL
I have...	**Tengo...**	TAYN-goh
...a boy friend.	**...un novio.**	oon NOH-bee-oh
...a girl friend.	**...una novia.**	OO-nah NOH-bee-ah
I am married.	**Estoy casado[a].**	ays-TOY kah-SAH-doh
I am not married.	**No estoy casado[a].**	noh ays-TOY kah-SAH-doh
I am rich and single.	**Soy rico[a] y soltero[a].**	soy REE-koh ee sohl-TAY-toh
I am lonely.	**Estoy solo[a].**	ays-TOY SOH-loh
I have no diseases.	**No tengo enfermedades.**	noh TAYN-goh ayn-fehr-may-DAH-days
I have many diseases.	**Tengo muchas enfermedades.**	TAYN-goh MOO-chahs ayn-fehr-may-DAH-days
Can I see you again?	**¿Te puedo volver a ver?**	tay PWAY-doh bohl-BEHR ah behr
You are my most beautiful souvenir.	**Tú eres mi mejor recuerdo.**	too AY-rays mee may-HOR ray-KWEHR-doh

Kiss me more.	**Bésame mucho.**	BAY-sah-may MOO-choh
Is this an aphrodisiac?	**¿Es esto un afrodisíaco?**	ays AYS-toh oon ah-froh-dee-SEE-ah-koh
This is (not) my first time.	**Esta (no) es mi primera vez.**	AYS-tah (noh) ays mee pree-MAY-rah bayth
Do you do this often?	**¿Haces esto muy a menudo?**	AH-thays AYS-toh MOO-ee ah may-NOO-doh
How's my breath?	**¿Me huele el aliento?**	may WAY-lay ehl ahl-YEHN-toh
Let's just be friends.	**Vamos a dejarlo como amigos.**	BAH-mohs ah day-HAR-loh KOH-moh ah-MEE-gohs
I'll pay for my share.	**Pagaré mi parte.**	pah-gah-RAY mee PAR-tay
Would you like a massage...?	**¿Te gustaría un masaje...?**	tay goo-stah-REE-ah oon mah-SAH-hay
...for your feet	**...por tus pies**	por toos pee-AYS
Why not?	**¿Por qué no?**	por kay noh
Try it.	**Pruébalo.**	proo-AY-bah-loh
It tickles.	**Esto me hace cosquillas.**	AYS-toh may AH-thay koh-SKEE-yahs
Oh my God.	**¡Dios mío!**	DEE-ohs MEE-oh
I love you.	**Te quiero.**	tay kee-EHR-oh
Darling, will you marry me?	**¿Querida, te casarás conmigo?**	kay-REE-dah tay kah-sah-RAHS kohn-MEE-goh

Getting Started

Portuguese
...is your passport to the land of sand and sun, sailors and seafood. Spanning the oceans, spoken from Brazil to Portugal to Mozambique, Portuguese is the portable language.

Here are a few peeks at pronouncing Portuguese words:

C usually sounds like C in cat.
　　But *C* followed by *E* or *I* sounds like S in sun.
Ç sounds like S in sun.
CH sounds like SH in shine.
G usually sounds like G in go.
　　But *G* followed by *E* or *I* sounds like S in treasure.
H is silent.
J sounds like S in treasure.
LH sounds like LI in billion.
NH sounds like NI in onion.
R is trrrilled.
S usually sounds like SH in shine.
　　But between vowels, *S* sounds like Z in zoo.
SS sounds like S in sun.

Portuguese vowels:

A can sound like A in father or A in sang.
E can sound like E in get, AY in play, or I in wish.
É sounds like E in get.
Ê sounds like AY in play.
I sounds like EE in seed.
O can sound like O in note, AW in raw, or OO in
    moon.
Ô and *OU* sound like O in note.
U sounds like OO in moon.

Portuguese has a few unusual signs. Some of the
vowels are topped with a ˜, such as *ã* and *õ*.
The ˜ can give the vowel a nasal sound, which we'll
discuss in a few paragraphs. Don't go away.

If a word ends in a vowel, the Portuguese usually
stress the second-to-last syllable. Words ending in a
consonant are stressed on the last syllable. To override
these rules, the Portuguese add an accent mark (such
as ´, ˜, or ^) to the syllable that should be stressed,
like this: *rápido* (fast) is pronounced RAH-pee-doo.

As with any Romance language, sex is important.
A man is *simpático* (friendly), a woman is *simpática*.
In this book, we show bi-sexual words like this:
simpático[a]. If you're speaking of a female

(which includes women speaking about themselves), use the *a* ending. It's always pronounced "ah." A word that ends in *r*, such as *cantor* (singer), will appear like this: *cantor[a]*. A *cantora* is a female singer. A word ending in *e*, such as *interessante* (interesting), applies to either sex. You'll be quizzed on this later.

Adjectives agree with the noun. A clean room is a *quarto limpo*, a clean towel is a *toalha limpa*.

Just like French, its linguistic buddy, Portuguese has nasal sounds. A vowel followed by either *n* or *m* or topped with ˜ is often nasalized. In the phonetics, nasalized vowels are indicated by an underlined **n** or **w**. As you say the vowel, let its sound come through your nose as well as your mouth.

Here are the phonetics for nasal vowels:

ay<u>n</u>	nasalize the AY in day.
oh<u>n</u>	nasalize the O in phone.
oo<u>n</u>	nazalize the O in moon.
o<u>w</u>	nasalize the OW in now.

Some words have only a slight nasal sound. To help you pronounce these words correctly, we add an *ng* or *n* in the phonetics: *sim* (yes) is pronounced seeng, and *muito* (very) like MWEEN-too.

Here's a quick guide to the rest of the phonetics we've used in this book:

a	like A in sang.
ah	like A in father.
ar	like AR in park.
aw	like AW in raw.
ay	like AY in play.
ee	like EE in seed.
eh	like E in get.
ehr	sounds like "air."
g	like G in go.
i	like I in hit.
ī	like I in light.
oh	like O in note.
oo	like OO in moon.
or	like OR in core.
ow	like OW in now.
oy	like OY in toy.
s	like S in sun.
zh	like S in treasure.

Too often, tourists insist on speaking Spanish to the Portuguese. Your attempts at Portuguese will endear you to the locals. And if you throw in *"por favor"* (please) whenever you can, you'll find the warmth of the people rivals that of the sun.

Portuguese Basics

Meeting and greeting the Portuguese:

Hello.	**Olá.**	oh-LAH
Good morning.	**Bom-dia.**	bohm-DEE-ah
Good afternoon.	**Boa-tarde.**	boh-ah-TAR-deh
Good evening.	**Boa-noite.**	boh-ah-NOY-teh
Mr.	**Senhor**	sin-YOR
Mrs.	**Senhora**	sin-YOH-rah
Miss	**Menina**	meh-NEE-nah
How are you?	**Como está?**	KOH-moo ish-TAH
Very well.	**Muito bem.**	MWEEN-too bayn
Thank you. (said by a male)	**Obrigado.**	oh-bree-GAH-doo
Thank you. (said by a female)	**Obrigada.**	oh-bree-GAH-dah
And you?	**E você?**	ee voh-SAY
My name is...	**Chamo-me...**	SHAH-moo-meh
What's your name?	**Como se chama?**	KOH-moo seh SHAH-mah
Pleased to meet you.	**Prazer em conhecer.**	prah-ZEHR ayn koon-yeh-SEHR
Where are you from?	**De onde é que você é?**	deh OHN-deh eh keh voh-SAY eh
I am... / Are you...?	**Estou... / Está...?**	ish-TOH / ish-TAH
...on vacation	**...de férias**	deh FEH-ree-ahsh

...on business	**...em negócios**	ayn neh-GAW-see-oosh
So long!	**Até logo!**	ah-TEH LAW-goo
Goodbye.	**Adeus.**	ah-DEH-oosh
Good luck!	**Boa sorte!**	BOH-ah SOR-teh
Have a good trip!	**Boa-viagem!**	boh-ah-vee-AH-zhayn

A woman who looks over 35 years old is addressed as *senhora*, younger than 35 as *menina*.

The Top 50 survival phrases

Yes, you can survive in Portugal using only these phrases. Most are repeated on your tear-out cheat sheet near the end of this book.

The ten essentials:

Hello.	**Olá.**	oh-LAH
Do you speak English?	**Fala inglês?**	FAH-lah een-GLAYSH
Yes.	**Sim.**	seeng
No.	**Não.**	now
I don't understand.	**Não compreendo.**	now kohm-pree-AYN-doo
I'm sorry.	**Desculpe.**	dish-KOOL-peh
Please.	**Por favor.**	poor fah-VOR
Thanks.	**Obrigado[a].**	oh-bree-GAH-doo

| Thank you very much. | **Muito obrigado[a].** | MWEEN-too oh-bree-GAH-doo |
| Goodbye. | **Adeus.** | ah-DEH-oosh |

Where?

Where is...?	**Onde é que é...?**	OHN-deh eh keh eh
...a hotel	**...um hotel**	oon oh-TEHL
...a youth hostel	**...uma pousada de juventude**	OO-mah poo-ZAH-dah deh zhoo-vayn-TOO-deh
...a restaurant	**...um restaurante**	oon rish-toh-RAHN-teh
...a grocery store	**...uma mercearia**	OO-mah mehr-see-ah-REE-ah
...the train station	**...a estação de comboio**	ah ish-tah-SOW deh kohm-BOY-yoo
...tourist information	**...a informação turistica**	ah een-for-mah-SOW too-REESH-tee-kah
...the toilet	**...a casa de banho**	ah KAH-zah deh BAHN-yoo
men / women	**homens / mulheres**	AW-maynsh / mool-YEH-rehsh

How much?

How much does it cost?	**Quanto custa?**	KWAHN-too KOOSH-tah
Write it, please.	**Escreva, por favor.**	ish-KRAY-vah poor fah-VOR
Cheap.	**Barato.**	bah-RAH-too
Cheaper.	**Mais barato.**	mīsh bah-RAH-too
Is it included?	**Está incluido?**	ish-TAH een-kloo-EE-doo
I would like...	**Gostaria...**	goosh-tah-REE-ah
We would like...	**Gostaríamos...**	goosh-tah-REE-ah-moosh
Just a little.	**Só um bocadinho.**	saw oon boo-kah-DEEN-yoo
More.	**Mais.**	mīsh
A ticket.	**Um bilhete.**	oon beel-YEH-teh
A room.	**Um quarto.**	oon KWAR-too
The bill.	**A conta.**	ah KOHN-tah

Number crunching:

one	**um**	oon
two	**dois**	doysh
three	**três**	traysh
four	**quatro**	KWAH-troo
five	**cinco**	SEENG-koo
six	**seis**	saysh
seven	**sete**	SEH-teh

eight	**oito**	OY-too
nine	**nove**	NAW-veh
ten	**dez**	dehsh

Moving on:

I go to...	**Vou para...**	voh PAH-rah
We go to...	**Vamos para...**	VAH-moosh PAH-rah
today	**hoje**	OH-zheh
tomorrow	**amanhã**	ah-ming-YAH
departure	**partida**	par-TEE-dah
At what time?	**A que horas?**	ah keh OH-rahsh

What's up:

Excuse me. (to get attention)	**Desculpe.**	dish-KOOL-peh
Just a moment.	**Um momento.**	oon moo-MAYN-too
It's a problem.	**Isso é um problema.**	EE-soo eh oon proo-BLAY-mah
Very good.	**Muito bem.**	MWEEN-too bayn
Fantastic!	**Fantástico!**	fahn-TAHSH-tee-koo
You are very kind.	**Você é muito simpático[a].**	voh-SAY eh MWEEN-too seem-PAH-tee-koo

You can mix and match these 50 survival phrases to say: "Two tickets," or "Yes, thanks," or "Where is a cheap restaurant?" or "The bill, please."

Struggling with Portuguese:

Do you speak English?	**Fala inglês?**	FAH-lah een-GLAYSH
A teeny weeny bit?	**Um pouquinho?**	oon poh-KEEN-yoo
Please speak English.	**Por favor fale inglês.**	poor fah-VOR FAH-leh een-GLAYSH
You speak English well.	**Fala bem inglês.**	FAH-lah bayn een-GLAYSH
I don't speak Portuguese.	**Não falo português.**	now FAH-loo poor-too-GAYSH
I speak a little Portuguese.	**Falo um pouco em português.**	FAH-loo oon POH-koo ayn poor-too-GAYSH
I speak ten words in Portuguese.	**Falo dez palavras em português.**	FAH-loo dehsh pah-LAHV-rahsh ayn poor-too-GAYSH
I study Portuguese.	**Estudo português.**	ish-TOO-doo poor-too-GAYSH
Excuse...	**Desculpe...**	dish-KOOL-peh
Correct...	**Corriga...**	koo-REE-gah
...my pronunciation.	**...a minha pronúncia.**	ah MEEN-yah proo-NOON-see-ah
What is this in Portuguese?	**O que é isto em português?**	oo keh eh EESH-too ayn poor-too-GAYSH
Excuse me? (didn't hear)	**Desculpe?**	dish-KOOL-peh
Repeat.	**Repita.**	ray-PEE-tah
Speak slowly.	**Fale devagar.**	FAH-leh day-vah-GAR
Do you understand?	**Compreende?**	kohm-pree-AYN-deh

I understand.	**Compreendo.**	kohm-pree-AYN-doo
I don't understand.	**Não compreendo.**	now kohm-pree-AYN-doo
Write it, please.	**Escreva, por favor.**	ish-KRAY-vah poor fah-VOR
Does anybody here speak English?	**Alguém fala inglês?**	AHL-gayn FAH-lah een-GLAYSH

Common questions in Portuguese:

How much?	**Quanto custa?**	KWAHN-too KOOSH-tah
How many?	**Quantos?**	KWAHN-toosh
How long? (time)	**Quanto tempo?**	KWAHN-too TAYN-poo
How far?	**A que distância?**	ah keh deesh-TAHN-see-ah
How?	**Como?**	KOH-moo
Is it possible?	**É possível?**	eh poo-SEE-vehl
What?	**O quê?**	oo kay
What is that?	**O que é isso?**	oo keh eh EE-soo
What is better?	**O que é melhor?**	oo keh eh mil-YOR
When?	**Quando?**	KWAHN-doo
What time is it?	**Que horas são?**	keh AW-rahs sow
At what time?	**A que horas?**	ah keh AW-rahs
What time does this...?	**A que horas é que...?**	ah keh AW-rahs eh keh
...open	**...abre**	AH-breh

...close	...fecha	FAY-shah
Do you have...?	Você tem...?	voh-SAY tay<u>n</u>
Where is...?	Onde é...?	OHN-deh eh
Where are...?	Onde estão...?	OHN-deh ish-TO<u>W</u>
Who?	Quem?	kay<u>n</u>
Why?	Porquê?	poor-KAY
Why not?	Porque não?	poor-KAY no<u>w</u>

A sentence or even a word becomes a question if you ask it in a questioning tone. *"Isso é bom"* (It's good) becomes *"Isso é bom?"* (Is it good?)

Yin and yang:

cheap / expensive	barato / caro	bah-RAH-too / KAH-roo
big / small	grande / pequeno	GRAHN-deh / pay-KAY-noo
hot / cold	quente / frio	KAYN-teh / FREE-oo
open / closed	aberto / fechado	ah-BEHR-too / feh-SHAH-doo
entrance / exit	entrada / saída	ayn-TRAH-dah / sah-EE-dah
arrive / depart	chegar / partir	shay-GAR / par-TEER
early / late	cedo / tarde	SAY-doo / TAR-deh
soon / later	em breve / mais tarde	ay<u>n</u> BRAY-veh / mīsh TAR-deh
fast / slow	rápido / lento	RAH-pee-doo / LAYN-too

here / there	**aqui / ali**	ah-KEE / ah-LEE
near / far	**perto / longe**	PEHR-too / LOHN-zheh
good / bad	**bom / mau**	bohn / mow
best / worst	**melhor / pior**	mil-YOR / pee-YOR
a little / lots	**um pouco / muito**	oon POH-koo / MWEEN-too
more / less	**mais / menos**	mīsh / MAY-noosh
easy / difficult	**fácil / difícil**	FAH-seel / dee-FEE-seel
beautiful / ugly	**lindo / feio**	LEEN-doo / FAY-oo
smart / stupid	**esperto / estupido**	ish-PEHR-too / ish-TOO-pee-doo
vacant / occupied	**livre / ocupado**	LEE-vreh / oo-koo-PAH-doo
with / without	**com / sem**	kohn / sayn

Portuguese names for places:

Portugal	**Portugal**	poor-too-GAHL
Lisbon	**Lisboa**	leezh-BOH-ah
Spain	**Espanha**	ish-PAHN-yah
Morocco	**Marrocos**	mah-RAW-koosh
France	**França**	FRAHN-sah
Germany	**Alemanha**	ah-leh-MAHN-yah
United States	**Estados Unidos**	ish-TAH-doosh oo-NEE-doosh
world	**o mundo**	oo MOON-doo

Little words that are big in Portugal:

I	**eu**	EH-oo
you (formal)	**você**	voh-SAY
you (informal)	**tu**	too
he	**ele**	EH-leh
she	**ela**	EH-lah
we	**nós**	nawsh
and	**e**	ee
at	**á**	ah
but	**mas**	mahsh
by (via)	**via**	VEE-ah
for	**para**	PAH-rah
from	**de**	deh
not	**não**	now
now	**agora**	ah-GOH-rah
only	**só**	saw
or	**ou**	oh
that	**aquilo**	ah-KEE-loo
this	**isto**	EESH-too
to	**para**	PAH-rah
very	**muito**	MWEEN-too

Numbers

0	**zero**	ZEH-roo
1	**um**	oon
2	**dois**	doysh
3	**três**	traysh
4	**quatro**	KWAH-troo
5	**cinco**	SEENG-koo
6	**seis**	saysh
7	**sete**	SEH-teh
8	**oito**	OY-too
9	**nove**	NAW-veh
10	**dez**	dehsh
11	**onze**	OHN-zeh
12	**doze**	DOH-zeh
13	**treze**	TRAY-zeh
14	**catorze**	kah-TOR-zeh
15	**quinze**	KEEN-zeh
16	**dezasseis**	deh-zah-SAYSH
17	**dezassete**	deh-zah-SEH-teh
18	**dezoito**	deh-ZOY-too
19	**dezanove**	deh-zah-NAW-veh
20	**vinte**	VEEN-teh
21	**vinte e um**	VEEN-teh ee oon
22	**vinte e dois**	VEEN-teh ee doysh
23	**vinte e três**	VEEN-teh ee traysh
30	**trinta**	TREEN-tah

31	**trinta e um**	TREEN-tah ee oon
40	**quarenta**	kwah-RAYN-tah
41	**quarenta e um**	kwah-RAYN-tah ee oon
50	**cinquenta**	seeng-KWAYN-tah
60	**sessenta**	seh-SAYN-tah
70	**setenta**	seh-TAYN-tah
80	**oitenta**	oy-TAYN-tah
90	**noventa**	noo-VAYN-tah
100	**cem**	sayn
101	**cento e um**	SAYN-too ee oon
102	**cento e dois**	SAYN-too ee doysh
143	**cento e quarenta e três**	SAYN-too ee kwah-RAYN-tah ee traysh
200	**duzentos**	doo-ZAYN-toosh
1000	**mil**	meel
1994	**mil novecentos e noventa e quatro**	meel naw-veh-SAYN-toosh ee noo-VAYN-tah ee KWAH-troo
2000	**dois mil**	doysh meel
1,000,000	**um milhão**	oon mil-YOW
first	**primeiro**	pree-MAY-roo
second	**segundo**	seh-GOON-doo
third	**terceiro**	tehr-SAY-roo
half	**metade**	meh-TAH-deh
fifty percent	**cinquenta percento**	seeng-KWAYN-tah pehr-SAYN-too
number one	**número um**	NOO-may-roo oon

Money

Handy Portuguese money words:

bank	**banco**	BANG-koo
money	**dinheiro**	deen-YAY-roo
change money	**troca de dinheiro**	TROH-kah deh deen-YAY-roo
exchange	**troca**	TROH-kah
traveler's check	**cheques de viagem**	SHEH-keh deh vee-AH-zhayn
credit card	**cartão de crédito**	kar-TOW deh KREH-dee-too
cash advance	**avanço de dinheiro**	ah-VAN-soo deh deen-YAY-roo
transfer of money	**transferência**	trahnsh-feh-RAYN-see-ah
cash machine	**caixa automática**	KĪ-shah ow-too-MAH-tee-kah
cashier	**caixa**	KĪ-shah
receipt	**recibo**	reh-SEE-boo

There are about 140 escudos to the dollar. To figure out Portuguese prices in dollars, cover the last two zeros, and subtract roughly 33%. A price of 1000 escudos equals about $7.

Changing money in Portugal:

Can you change dollars?	**Pode trocar dollares?**	PAW-deh troo-KAR DAW-lah-rehsh
What is your exchange rate for dollars...?	**Qual é a taxa de câmbio para o dollar...?**	kwahl eh ah TAH-shah deh KAHM-bee-oo PAH-rah oo DAW-lar
...in traveler's checks	**...em cheque de viagem**	ayn SHEH-keh deh vee-AH-zhayn
Are there extra fees?	**À taxas extras?**	ah TAHSH-ahsh ISH-trahsh
What is...?	**O que é...?**	oo keh eh
...the service charge	**...a taxa de serviço**	ah TAH-shah deh sehr-VEE-soo
...the commission	**...a comissão**	ah koo-mee-SOW
I would like...	**Gostaria...**	goosh-teh-REE-ah
...small bills.	**...notas pequenas.**	NAW-tahsh peh-KAY-nahsh
...large bills.	**...notas grandes.**	NAW-tahsh GRAHN-dehsh
...coins.	**...moedas.**	moo-EH-dahsh
I think you've made a mistake.	**Acho que você fez um erro.**	AH-shoo keh voh-SAY faysh oon EH-roo
I'm broke.	**Estou teso[a].**	ish-TOH TAY-zoo

Public Transportation

Tickets:

ticket	**bilhete**	beel-YEH-teh
ticket office	**bilheteira**	beel-yeh-TAY-rah
schedule	**horário**	aw-RAH-ree-oo
one way	**uma ida**	OO-mah EE-dah
roundtrip	**ida e volta**	EE-dah ee VOHL-tah
overnight	**pernoitar**	pehr-noy-TAR
direct	**directo**	dee-REH-too
connection	**conexão**	koh-nehk-SOW
express service	**expresso**	ish-PREH-soo
first class	**primeira classe**	pree-MAY-rah KLAH-seh
second class	**segunda classe**	seh-GOON-dah KLAH-seh
reservation	**reserva**	ray-ZEHR-vah
seat...	**lugar...**	loo-GAR
...window	**...à janela**	ah zhah-NEH-lah
...aisle	**...sobre corredor**	SOH-breh koo-ray-DOR'
non-smoking	**não fumador**	now foo-mah-DOR
refund	**reembolso**	reh-ayn-BOHL-soo

At the station:

arrival	**chegada**	shay-GAH-dah
departure	**partida**	par-TEE-dah
delay	**atrazo**	ah-TRAH-zoo
waiting room	**sala de espera**	SAH-lah deh ish-PEH-rah
lockers	**depósito de bagagem automático**	deh-PAW-zee-too deh bah-GAH-zhayn ow-too-MAH-tee-koo
baggage	**bagagem**	bah-GAH-zhayn
baggage check room	**despacho de bagagem**	dish-PAH-shoo deh bah-GAH-zhayn
lost and found office	**perdidos e achados**	pehr-DEE-doosh ee ah-SHAH-doosh
tourist information	**informação turistica**	een-for-mah-SOW too-REESH-tee-kah

Trains:

Portuguese State Railways	**Caminhos de Ferro**	kah-MEEN-yoosh deh FEHR-roo
train station	**estação de comboio**	ish-tah-SOW deh kohm-BOY-yoo
train information	**informação sobre comboios**	een-for-mah-SOW SOH-breh kohm-BOY-yoosh
train	**comboio**	kohm-BOY-yoo

high-speed train	**expresso**	ish-PREH-soo
to the platforms	**acesso ão cais**	ah-SEH-soo o<u>w</u> kīsh
platform	**cais**	kīsh
track	**linha**	LEEN-yah
train car	**carruagem**	kar-WAH-zhay<u>n</u>
dining car	**carruagem restaurante**	kar-WAH-zhay<u>n</u> rish-toh-RAHN-teh
sleeper car	**carruagem cama**	kar-WAH-zhay<u>n</u> KAH-mah
sleeper berth	**beliche**	beh-LEE-sheh
conductor	**condutor**	kohn-doo-TOR

Buses:

bus station	**terminal das camionetas**	tehr-mee-NAHL dahsh kahm-yoo-NEH-tahsh
long-distance bus	**camioneta**	kahm-yoo-NEH-tah
city bus	**autocarro**	ow-too-KAH-roo
bus stop	**paragem de autocarro**	pah-RAH-zhay<u>n</u> deh ow-too-KAH-roo

Portuguese transportation phrases:

How much is the fare to...?	**Quanto custa o bilhete para...?**	KWAHN-too KOOSH-tah oo beel-YEH-teh PAH-rah
I'd like...	**Gostaria...**	goosh-tah-REE-ah
...to go to ___.	**...de ir para ___.**	day eer PAH-rah

...a ticket to ___.	...um bilhete para ___.	oon beel-YEH-teh PAH-rah
Is a reservation required?	É preciso reservar?	eh preh-SEE-zoo ray-zehr-VAR
I'd like to leave...	Gostaria de ir embora...	goosh-tah-REE-ah deh eer aym-BOH-rah
I'd like to arrive...	Gostaria de chegar...	goosh-tah-REE-ah deh shay-GAR
...by ___. (time)	...por ___.	poor
...in the morning.	...de manhã.	deh ming-YAH
...in the afternoon.	...de tarde.	deh TAR-deh
...in the evening.	...ao anoitecer.	ow ah-noy-teh-SEHR
Is there...?	Será que à...?	seh-RAH keh ah
...an earlier departure	...uma partida mais cedo	OO-mah par-TEE-dah mīsh SAY-doo
...a later departure	...uma partida mais tarde	OO-mah par-TEE-dah mīsh TAR-deh
...a supplement	...um suplemento	oon soo-pleh-MAYN-too
...a cheaper ticket	...um bilhete mais barato	oon beel-YEH-teh mīsh bah-RAH-too
When is the next departure?	Quando é a próxima partida?	KWAHN-doo eh ah PRAW-see-mah par-TEE-dah
Write it, please.	Escreva, por favor.	ish-KRAY-vah poor fah-VOR
Where does it leave from?	De onde é que parte?	deh OHN-deh eh keh PAR-teh

On what track?	**Em que linha?**	ayn keh LEEN-yah
When will it arrive?	**Quando é que vai chegar?**	KWAHN-doo eh keh vī shay-GAR
Is it direct?	**É directo?**	eh dee-REH-too
Must I transfer?	**É preciso mudar?**	eh preh-SEE-zoo moo-DAR
When? / Where?	**Quando? / Onde?**	KWAHN-doo / OHN-deh
Which train to...?	**Que comboio para...?**	keh kohm-BOY-yoo PAH-rah
Which bus to...?	**Que autocarro para...?**	keh ow-too-KAH-roo PAH-rah
Does it stop at...?	**Para em...?**	PAH-rah ayn
Is this (seat) free?	**Está livre?**	ish-TAH LEE-vreh
That's my seat.	**Este é o meu lugar.**	AYSH-teh eh oo MEH-oo loo-GAR
Save my place.	**Guarde o meu lugar.**	GWAR-deh oo MEH-oo loo-GAR
Where are you going?	**Onde é que vai?**	OHN-deh eh keh vī
I go to...	**Vou para...**	voh PAH-rah
Can you tell me when to get off?	**Pode-me dizer quando é que preciso sair?**	PAW-deh-meh dee-ZEHR KWAHN-doo eh keh preh-SEE-zoo sah-EER

Reading Portuguese train and bus schedules:

até	until
chegada	arrival
de	from
diário	daily
dias	days
dias da semana	weekdays
domingo	Sunday
domingos e feriados	Sundays and holidays
excepto	except
feriado	holiday
para	to
partida	departure
sabádo	Saturday
só	only
todo	every

Taking taxis in Portugal:

Where can I get a taxi?	**Onde posso apanhar um táxi?**	OHN-deh PAW-soo ah-pahn-YAR oon TAHK-see
Are you free?	**Está livre?**	ish-TAH LEE-vreh
Occupied.	**Ocupado.**	oo-koo-PAH-doo
How much will it cost to go to...?	**Quanto é que custa a viagem para...?**	KWAHN-too eh keh KOOSH-tah ah vee-AH-zhayn PAH-rah
Too much.	**É muito caro.**	eh MWEEN-too KAH-roo

English	Portuguese	Pronunciation
How many people can you take?	**Quantas pessoas é que pode levar?**	KWAHN-tahsh peh-SOH-ahsh eh keh PAW-deh leh-VAR
Is there an extra fee?	**À alguma taxa extra?**	ah ahl-GOO-mah TAH-shah ISH-trah
The meter, please.	**O medidor, por favor.**	oo may-dee-DOR poor fah-VOR
The most direct route.	**O caminho mais direto.**	oo kah-MEEN-yoo mīsh dee-REH-too
Slow down.	**Mais devagar.**	mīsh day-vah-GAR
If you don't slow down, I'll throw up.	**Se não for mais devagar, vou vomitar.**	seh now for mīsh day-vah-GAR voh voo-mee-TAR
Stop here.	**Pare aqui.**	PAH-rah ah-KEE
Can you wait?	**Pode esperar?**	PAW-deh ish-peh-RAR
I'll never forget this ride.	**Nunca vou esquecer esta viagem.**	NOON-kah voh ish-keh-SEHR EHSH-tah vee-AH-zhayn
Where did you learn to drive?	**Onde é que aprendeu a conduzir?**	OHN-deh eh keh ah-PRAYND-yoo ah kohn-doo-ZEER
I'll only pay what's on the meter.	**Só pago o que o medidor diz.**	saw PAH-goo oo keh oo may-dee-DOR deesh
My change, please.	**O meu troco, por favor.**	oo MEH-oo TROH-koo poor fah-VOR
Keep the change.	**Fique com o troco.**	FEE-keh kohn oo TROH-koo

Driving

Wheeling and dealing:

I'd like to rent...	**Gostaria de alugar...**	goosh-tah-REE-ah deh ah-loo-GAR
...a car.	**...um carro.**	oon KAH-roo
...a motorcycle.	**...uma mota.**	OO-mah MOH-tah
...a motor scooter.	**...uma motocicleta.**	OO-mah moh-toh-see-KLEH-tah
...a bicycle.	**...uma bicicleta.**	OO-mah bee-see-KLEH-tah
...a secluded beach.	**...uma praia isolada.**	OO-mah PRĪ-ah ee-zoo-LAH-dah
How much...?	**Quanto custa...?**	KWAHN-too KOOSH-tah
...per hour	**...á hora**	ah AW-rah
...per day	**...ao dia**	ow DEE-ah
...per week	**...á semana**	ah seh-MAH-nah

Rather than dollars and gallons, gas pumps in Portugal will read escudos and liters (basically 140 escudos in a dollar, and 4 liters in a gallon). Drive carefully. Statistically, Portugal's roads are the most dangerous in Europe.

Gassing up in Portugal:

gas station	**bomba de gasolina**	BOHM-bah deh gah-zoo-LEE-nah
The nearest gas station?	**A próxima bomba de gasolina?**	ah PRAW-see-mah BOHM-bah deh gah-zoo-LEE-nah
Is it self-service?	**É self-service?**	eh "self-service"
Fill the tank.	**Abastecer o carro.**	ah-bahsh-teh-SEHR oo KAH-roo
I need...	**Preciso...**	preh-SEE-zoo
...gas.	**...gasolina.**	gah-zoo-LEE-nah
...unleaded.	**...sem chumbo.**	sayn SHOOM-boo
...regular.	**...normal.**	nor-MAHL
...super.	**...super.**	soo-PEHR
...diesel.	**...diesel.**	dee-ZEHL
Check...	**Verificar...**	veh-ree-fee-KAR
...the oil.	**...o óleo.**	oo AWL-yoo
...the air in the tires.	**...o ar nos pneus.**	oo ar noosh PEHN-yoosh
...the water.	**...o água.**	oo AH-gwah
...the radiator.	**...o radiador.**	oo rah-dee-ah-DOR
...the battery.	**...a bateria.**	ah bah-teh-REE-ah
...the brakes.	**...os travões.**	oosh trah-VOHNSH
...my pulse.	**...a minha pulsação.**	ah MEEN-yah pool-sah-SOW

Portuguese car trouble:

accident	**acidente**	ah-see-DAYN-teh
breakdown	**parado**	pah-RAH-doo
funny noise	**barulho estranho**	bah-ROOL-yoo ish-TRAHN-yoo
electrical problem	**problema elétrico**	proo-BLAY-mah eh-LEH-tree-koo
My car won't start.	**O meu carro não arranca.**	oo MEH-oo KAH-roo now ah-RAHN-kah
This doesn't work.	**Isto não trabalha.**	EESH-too now trah-BAHL-yah
It's overheating.	**Está muito quente.**	ish-TAH MWEEN-too KAYN-teh
I need...	**Preciso...**	preh-SEE-zoo
...a tow truck.	**...um reboque.**	oon reh-BAW-keh
...a mechanic.	**...um mecânico.**	oon meh-KAHN-nee-koo
...a stiff drink.	**...uma bebida forte.**	OO-mah beh-BEE-dah FOR-teh
Can you fix it?	**Pode reparar isto?**	PAW-deh reh-pah-RAR EESH-too
Just do the essentials.	**Faça só o que for preciso.**	FAH-sah saw oo keh for preh-SEE-zoo
When will it be ready?	**Quando é que vai estar pronto?**	KWAHN-doo eh keh vī ish-TAR PROHN-too

| How much will it cost to make it run? | **Quanto é que vai custar para funcioanar de novo?** | KWAHN-too eh keh vī koosh-TAR PAH-rah foon-see-oh-NAR deh NOH-voo |
| I'm going to faint. | **Vou desmaiar.** | voh dish-mī-YAR |

Parking in Portugal:

parking garage	**garagem**	gah-RAH-zhay<u>n</u>
Where can I park?	**Onde é que posso estacionar?**	OHN-deh eh keh PAW-soo ish-tah-see-oo-NAR
Is parking nearby?	**É perto do estacionamento?**	eh PEHR-too doo ish-tah-see-oo-nah-MAYN-too
Can I park here?	**Posso fazer parking aqui?**	PAW-soo fah-ZEHR par-KEENG ah-KEE
How long can I park here?	**Quanto tempo posso estacionar aqui?**	KWAHN-too TAY<u>N</u>-poo PAW-soo ish-tah-see-oo-NAR ah-KEE
Must I pay to park here?	**É preciso pagar para estacionar aqui?**	eh preh-SEE-zoo pah-GAR PAH-rah ish-tah-see-oo-NAR ah-KEE
Is this a safe place to park?	**É seguro estacionar aqui?**	eh say-GOO-roo ish-tah-see-oo-NAR ah-KEE

Finding Your Way

Key Portuguese navigation words:

straight ahead	**em frente**	ay<u>n</u> FRAYN-teh
left / right	**esquerda / direita**	ish-KEHR-dah / dee-RAY-tah
first / next	**primeira / próximo**	pree-MAY-rah / PRAW-see-moo
intersection	**cruzamento**	kroo-zah-MAYN-too
stoplight	**sinal de luz**	see-NAHL deh loosh
square	**praça**	PRAH-sah
street	**rua**	ROO-ah
bridge	**ponte**	POHN-teh
tunnel	**túnel**	TOO-nehl
overpass	**sobre a estrada**	SOH-breh ah ish-TRAH-dah
underpass	**debaixo da estrada**	deh-BĪ-shoo dah ish-TRAH-dah
highway	**autoestrada**	ow-too-ish-TRAH-dah
map	**mapa**	MAH-pah

Getting directions in Portugal:

I go to...	**Vou para...**	voh PAH-rah
How do I get to...?	**Como é que vou para...?**	KOH-moo eh keh voh PAH-rah
How many minutes...?	**Quantos minutos para...?**	KWAHN-toosh mee-NOO-toosh PAH-rah
...on foot	**...a caminhar**	ah kah-meen-YAR
...by car	**...a conduzir**	ah kohn-doo-ZEER
How many kilometers to...?	**Quantos kilómetros para...?**	KWAHN-toosh kee-LAW-meh-troosh PAH-rah
What's the... route to Faro?	**Qual é... estrada para Faro?**	kwahl eh... ish-TRAH-dah PAH-rah FAH-roo
...best	**...a melhor**	ah mil-YOR
...fastest	**...a mais rápida**	ah mīsh RAH-pee-dah
...most interesting	**...a mais interessante**	ah mīsh een-teh-reh-SAHN-teh
Show me on this map.	**Mostre-me neste mapa.**	MOHSH-treh-meh NAYSH-teh MAH-pah
I'm lost.	**Estou perdido[a].**	ish-TOH pehr-DEE-doo
Where am I?	**Onde é que estou?**	OHN-deh eh keh ish-TOH
Who am I?	**Quem é que sou?**	kayn eh keh soh
Where is...?	**Onde é que é...?**	OHN-deh eh keh eh
The nearest...?	**O próximo...?**	oo PRAW-see-moo
Where is this address?	**Onde é este endereço?**	OHN-deh eh AYSH-teh ayn-deh-RAY-soo

Reading Portuguese road signs:

abrandar	yield
baixa	to the center of town
construção na estrada	workers ahead
cuidado	caution
desvio	detour
devagar	slow
entrada	entrance
estacionamento proibido	no parking
pare	stop
peões	pedestrians
saída	exit
sentido único	one-way street

Other Portuguese signs you may bump into:

aberto das... ás...	open from... to...
água não potável	undrinkable water
casa de banho / WC	toilet
fechado para férias	closed for vacation
fechado para restauração	closed for restoration
homens / mulheres	men / women
ocupado	occupied
para alugar / venda	for rent / sale
perigo	danger
proibido	forbidden
proíbida a entrada	no entry
proibido fumar	no smoking
saída de emergência	emergency exit
Turismo	tourist information office

Telephones

Key Portuguese telephone words:

post (& telephone) office	**correios**	koo-RAY-oosh
telephone	**telefone**	teh-leh-FAW-neh
operator	**telefonista**	teh-leh-faw-NEESH-tah
international assistance	**assistência internacional**	ah-seesh-TAYN-see-ah een-tehr-nah-see-oo-NAHL
country code	**código do país**	KAW-dee-goo doo pah-EESH
area code	**código da area**	KAW-dee-goo dah ah-RAY-ah
phone card	**cartão telefónico**	kar-TOW teh-leh-FAW-nee-koo
telephone book	**lista telefónica**	LEESH-tah teh-leh-FAW-nee-kah
yellow pages	**páginas amarelas**	PAH-zhee-nahsh ah-mah-REH-lahsh
toll-free	**taxa grátis**	TAH-shah GRAH-teesh
out of service	**desligado**	dish-lee-GAH-doo

Handy Portuguese phone phrases:

The nearest phone?	O próximo telefone?	oo PRAW-see-moo teh-leh-FAW-neh
It doesn't work.	Não funciona.	now foon-see-OH-nah
Where is the post office?	Onde é que são os correios?	OHN-deh eh keh sow oosh koo-RAY-oosh
I'd like to telephone...	Gostaria de telefonar...	goosh-tah-REE-ah deh teh-leh-faw-NAR
...the United States.	...para os Estados Unidos.	PAH-rah oosh ish-TAH-doosh oo-NEE-doosh
How much per minute?	Quanto custa por minuto?	KWAHN-too KOOSH-tah poor mee-NOO-too
I'd like to make a... call.	Gostaria de fazer uma chamada...	goosh-tah-REE-ah deh fah-ZEER OO-mah shah-MAH-dah
...local	...local.	loo-KAHL
...collect	...à cobrança.	ah koo-BRAN-sah
...credit card	...com o meu cartão de crédito.	kohn oo MEH-oo kar-TOW deh KRAY-dee-too
...person to person	...pessõalmente.	peh-soo-ahl-MAYN-teh
...long distance (within Portugal)	...para fora da cidade.	PAH-rah FOH-rah dah see-DAH-deh
...international	...internacional.	een-tehr-nah-see-oo-NAHL
...fax	...fax.	"fax"

May I use your phone?	**Posso utilizar o seu telefone?**	PAW-soo oo-tee-lee-ZAR oo SEH-oo teh-leh-FAW-neh
Can you dial for me?	**Pode fazer a ligação por mim?**	PAW-deh fah-ZEHR ah lee-gah-SOW poor meeng
Can you talk for me?	**Pode falar por mim?**	PAW-deh fah-LAR poor meeng
It's busy.	**Está ocupado.**	ish-TAH oo-koo-PAH-doo
Will you try again?	**Pode tentar novamente?**	PAW-deh tayn-TAR noo-vah-MAYN-teh
Hello. (on phone)	**Está.**	ish-TAH
My name is...	**O meu nome é...**	oo MEH-oo NOH-meh eh
My number is...	**O meu número é...**	oo MEH-oo NOO-may-roo eh
Speak slowly and clearly.	**Fale devagar e claramente.**	FAH-leh day-vah-GAR ee klah-rah-MAYN-teh
Wait a moment.	**Um momento.**	oon moo-MAYN-too
Don't hang up.	**Não desligue.**	now dish-LEE-geh

You can make your calls at a phone booth or the post office (*correios*). In a phone booth, insert the handy phone card (*cartão telefónico*) into the phone instead of coins to make your calls. See "Telephone Talk" near the end of this book for more phone tips.

Finding a Room

If you keep it very simple and use these phrases, you will be able to reserve a hotel room over the phone. A good time to reserve a room is the morning of the day you plan to arrive. Related words and phrases can be found in the Telephone and Time sections.

Key Portuguese room-finding words:

hotel	**hotel**	oh-TEHL
family-run hotel	**pensão, residência**	payn-SOW, reh-zee-DEHN-see-ah
fancy historic hotel	**pousada**	poh-ZAH-dah
room in private home	**quarto**	KWAR-too
youth hostel	**pousada de juventude**	poo-ZAH-dah deh zhoo-vayn-TOO-deh
room	**quarto**	KWAR-too
people	**pessoas**	peh-SOH-ahsh
night	**noite**	NOY-teh
arrive	**chegada**	shay-GAH-dah
today	**hoje**	OH-zheh
tomorrow	**amanhã**	ah-ming-YAH
vacancy sign (literally "rooms")	**quartos**	KWAR-toosh

Handy Portuguese hotel-hunting phrases:

I'd like to reserve a room...	**Gostaria de reservar um quarto...**	goosh-tah-REE-ah deh ray-zehr-VAR oon KWAR-too
Do you have a room for...?	**Tem um quarto para...?**	tayn oon KWAR-too PAH-rah
...one person / two people	**...uma pessoa / duas pessoas**	OO-mah peh-SOH-ah / DOO-ahsh peh-SOH-ahsh
...tonight	**...esta noite**	EHSH-tah NOY-teh
...two nights	**...duas noites**	DOO-ahsh NOY-tehsh
...this Monday night	**...esta segunda-feira à noite**	EHSH-tah seh-goon-dah-FAY-rah ah NOY-teh
...Monday, August 28	**...segunda-feira, dia 28 de Agosto**	seh-goon-dah-FAY-rah, DEE-ah VEEN-teh ee OY-too deh ah-GOHSH-too
with / without / and	**com / sem / e**	kohn / sayn / ee
...a toilet	**...uma casa de banho**	OO-mah KAH-zah deh BAHN-yoo
...a shower	**...um chuveiro**	oon shoo-VAY-roo
...a private bathroom	**...uma casa de banho privada**	OO-mah KAH-zah deh BAHN-yoo pree-VAH-dah
...a double bed	**...uma cama grande**	OO-mah KAH-mah GRAHN-deh

...twin beds	**...camas gémeas**	KAH-mahsh
		ZHEH-meh-ahsh
...view	**...vista**	VEESH-tah
with only a sink	**só com um**	saw kohn oon
	lavatório	lah-vah-TAW-ree-oo
How much	**Quanto custa?**	KWAHN-too
does it cost?		KOOSH-tah

You may hear: *"Desculpe"* (I'm sorry). *"Não tenho vaga"* (No vacancy). Or, *"Você precisa de chegar antes das quatro da tarde."* (You must arrive before 4:00 in the afternoon).

Working out the details:

My name is...	**O meu nome é...**	oo MEH-oo
		NOH-meh eh
I'm coming now.	**Estou a chegar**	ish-TOH ah shay-GAR
	agora.	ah-GOH-rah
I'll arrive in	**Vou chegar dentro**	voh shay-GAR
one hour.	**de uma hora.**	DAYN-troo deh
		OO-mah AW-rah
I'll arrive before 4:00	**Vou chegar antes**	voh shay-GAR AHN-
in the afternoon.	**das quatro da tarde.**	tehsh dahsh KWAH-
		troo deh TAR-deh
We arrive Monday,	**Vamos chegar**	VAH-moosh shay-GAR
depart Wednesday.	**segunda-feira, e**	seh-goon-dah-FAY-rah,
	partir quarta-feira.	ee par-TEER
		kwar-tah-FAY-rah

I have a reservation.	**Tenho reserva.**	TAYN-yoo ray-ZEHR-vah
Confirm my reservation.	**Confirmar a minha reserva.**	kohm-feer-MAR ah MEEN-yah ray-ZEHR-vah
I'll sleep anywhere.	**Dormo em qualquer lugar.**	DOR-moo ayn kwahl-KEHR loo-GAR
I have a sleeping bag.	**Tenho um saco de cama.**	TAYN-yoo oon SAH-koo deh KAH-mah
How much is your cheapest room?	**Quanto custa o seu quarto mais barato?**	KWAHN-too KOOSH-tah oo SEH-oo KWAR-too mīsh bah-RAH-too
Is it cheaper if I stay three nights?	**É mais barato se ficar três noites?**	eh mīsh bah-RAH-too seh fee-KAR traysh NOY-tehsh
I will stay three nights.	**Vou ficar três noites.**	voh fee-KAR traysh NOY-tehsh
Breakfast included?	**Pequeno almoço incluído?**	peh-KAY-noo ahl-MOH-soo een-kloo-EE-doo
How much without breakfast?	**Quanto custa sem o pequeno almoço?**	KWAHN-too KOOSH-tah sayn oo peh-KAY-noo ahl-MOH-soo
Complete price?	**Preço total?**	PRAY-soo too-TAHL
Service included?	**O serviço está incluído?**	oo sehr-VEE-soo ish-TAH een-kloo-EE-doo
Can I see the room?	**Posso ver o quarto?**	PAW-soo vehr oo KWAR-too
Show me another room.	**Mostre-me outro quarto.**	MOHSH-treh-meh OH-troo KWAR-too

Do you have something...?	**Tem alguma coisa...?**	tayn ahl-GOO-mah KOY-zah
...larger / smaller	**...maior / pequeno**	mī-YOR / peh-KAY-noo
...better / cheaper	**...melhor / barato**	mil-YOR / bah-RAH-too
...in the back	**...nas traseiras**	nahsh trah-ZAY-rahsh
...quieter	**...calmo**	KAHL-moo
No, thank you.	**Não, obrigado[a].**	now oh-bree-GAH-doo
Very good.	**Muito bem.**	MWEEN-too bayn
I'll take this room.	**Fico com este quarto.**	FEE-koo kohn AYSH-teh KWAR-too
My key, please.	**A minha chave, por favor.**	ah MEEN-yah SHAH-veh poor fah-VOR
Sleep well.	**Dorme bem.**	DOR-meh bayn
Good night.	**Boa-noite.**	boh-ah-NOY-teh

Portuguese hotel help and hassles:

I'd like...	**Gostaria...**	goosh-tah-REE-ah
...clean sheets.	**...lençóis limpos.**	LAYN-soysh LEEM-poosh
...a pillow.	**...uma almofada.**	OO-mah ahl-moo-FAH-dah
...a blanket.	**...um cobertor.**	oon koo-behr-TOR
...a towel.	**...uma toalha.**	OO-mah too-AHL-yah
...toilet paper.	**...papel higiénico.**	pah-PEHL ee-zhee-EHN-ee-koo

...a small extra bed.	**...uma pequena cama extra.**	OO-mah peh-KAY-nah KAH-mah ISH-trah
...silence.	**...silêncio.**	see-LAYN-see-oo
Is there an elevator?	**Tem elevador?**	tayn eh-leh-vah-DOR
Come with me.	**Venha comigo.**	VAYN-yah koo-MEE-goo
I have a problem in my room.	**Tenho um problema no meu quarto.**	TAYN-yoo oon proo-BLAY-mah noo MEH-oo KWAR-too
bad odor	**cheira mal**	SHAY-rah mahl
bugs	**insectos**	een-SEH-toosh
mice	**rato**	RAH-too
prostitutes	**prostitutas**	proosh-tee-TOO-tahsh
The bed is too soft / hard.	**Esta cama é muito mole / dura.**	EHSH-tah KAH-mah eh MWEEN-too MAW-leh / DOO-rah
There is no hot water.	**Não hà água quente.**	now ah AH-gwah KAYN-teh
When is the water hot?	**Quando hà água quente?**	KWAHN-doo ah AH-gwah KAYN-teh
Where can I wash my laundry?	**Onde é que posso lavar a minha roupa?**	OHN-deh eh keh PAW-soo lah-VAR ah MEEN-yah ROH-pah
I'd like to stay another night.	**Gostaria de ficar outra noite.**	goosh-tah-REE-ah deh fee-KAR OH-trah NOY-teh
Where shall I park?	**Onde é que estaciono?**	OHN-deh eh keh ish-tah-see-OH-noo

What time do you lock up?	**A que horas fecha?**	ah keh AW-rahsh FAY-shah
What time is breakfast?	**A que horas é o pequeno almoço?**	ah keh AW-rahsh eh oo peh-KAY-noo ahl-MOH-soo
Wake me at 7:00.	**Acorde-me ás sete da manhã.**	ah-KOR-deh-meh ahsh SEH-teh dah ming-YAH

Checking out in Portugal:

I'll / We'll leave...	**Vou / Vamos sair ás...**	voh / VAH-moosh sah-EER ahsh
...today / tomorrow.	**...hoje / amanhã.**	OH-zheh / ah-ming-YAH
When is check-out time?	**A que horas é preciso pagar a conta e sair?**	ah keh AW-rahsh eh preh-SEE-zoo pah-GAR ah KOHN-tah ee SAH-eer
Can I pay now?	**Posso pagar agora?**	PAW-soo pah-GAR ah-GOR-ah
The bill, please.	**A conta, por favor.**	ah KOHN-tah poor fah-VOR
Do you accept a credit card?	**Aceita cartão de crédito?**	ah-SAY-tah kar-TOW deh KRAY-dee-too
Everything was great.	**Tudo foi óptimo.**	TOO-doo foy AWP-tee-moo
Can I leave my bag until...?	**Posso deixar o meu saco até ás...?**	PAW-soo day-SHAR oo MEH-oo SAH-koo ah-TEH ahsh

Eating

Finding a restaurant in Portugal:

Where's a good... restaurant?	**Onde hà um bom restaurante...?**	OHN-deh ah oon bohn rish-toh-RAHN-teh
...cheap	**...barato**	bah-RAH-too
...local-style	**...estilo regional**	ish-TEE-loo ray-zhee-oh-NAHL
...untouristy	**...não turistico**	now too-REESH-tee-koo
...Chinese	**...chinês**	shee-NAYSH
...fast food	**...comida rápida**	koo-MEE-dah RAH-pee-dah

Ordering meals in Portuguese:

What would you like?	**O que é que gostaria?**	oo keh eh keh goosh-tah-REE-ah
I'd like...	**Gostaria...**	goosh-tah-REE-ah
...a table for two.	**...uma mesa para duas pessoas.**	OO-mah MAY-zah PAH-rah DOO-ahsh peh-SOH-ahsh
...non-smoking.	**...não fumador.**	now foo-mah-DOR
...just a drink.	**...só uma bebida.**	saw OO-mah beh-BEE-dah
...a tourist menu.	**...uma ementa turistica.**	OO-mah ah-MAYN-tah too-REESH-tee-kah
...a snack.	**...um petisco.**	oon peh-TEESH-koo

...a half portion.	**...meia dose.**	MAY-ah DOH-zeh
...to see the menu.	**...de ver a amenta.**	deh vehr ah ah-MAYN-tah
...to order.	**...encomendar.**	ayn-koo-mayn-DAR
...to eat.	**...de comer.**	deh koo-MEHR
...to pay.	**...de pagar.**	deh pah-GAR
...to throw up.	**...de vomitar.**	deh voo-mee-TAR
What do you recommend?	**O que é que recomenda?**	oo keh eh keh ray-koo-MAYN-dah
What's your favorite?	**Qual é a sua comida favorita?**	kwahl eh ah SOO-ah koo-MEE-dah fah-voo-REE-tah
Is it...?	**Isto é...?**	EESH-too eh
...good	**...bom**	boh<u>n</u>
...expensive	**...caro**	KAH-roo
...light	**...leve**	LEH-veh
...filling	**...para encher**	PAH-rah ayn-SHEHR
What's local?	**O que é da região?**	oo keh eh dah rayzh-YO<u>W</u>
What is...?	**O que é...?**	oo keh eh
...that	**...aquilo**	ah-KEE-loo
...fast	**...rápido**	RAH-pee-doo
...cheap and filling	**...barato e enche**	bah-RAH-too ee AYN-sheh
Do you have...?	**Você tem...?**	voh-SAY tay<u>n</u>
...an English menu	**...uma ementa em inglês**	OO-mah ah-MAYN-tah ay<u>n</u> een-GLAYSH
...a children's portion	**...uma refeição para criança**	OO-mah reh-fay-SO<u>W</u> PAH-rah kree-AHN-sah

Dietary restrictions:

I'm allergic to...	**Sou alérgico[a] a...**	soh ah-LEHR-zhee-koo ah
I cannot eat...	**Não posso comer...**	now PAW-soo koo-MEHR
...dairy products.	**...produtos lácteos.**	proo-DOO-toosh LAHK-teh-oosh
...fat.	**...gordura.**	gor-DOO-rah
...meat.	**...carne.**	KAR-neh
...salt.	**...sal.**	sahl
...sugar.	**...açúcar.**	ah-SOO-kar
I am diabetic.	**Sou diabético[a].**	soh dee-ah-BEH-tee-koo
No alcohol.	**Não alcool.**	now AHL-kahl
I am a...	**Sou...**	soh
...vegetarian.	**...vegetariano[a].**	veh-zheh-tar-ree-AH-noo
...strict vegetarian.	**...rigorosamente vegetariano[a].**	ree-goh-roh-zah-MAYN-teh veh-zheh-tar-ree-AH-noo
...carnivore.	**...carnivoro[a].**	kar-nee-VOH-roo

Key Portuguese menu words:

breakfast	**pequeno almoço**	peh-KAY-noo ahl-MOH-soo
lunch	**almoço**	ahl-MOH-soo

dinner	**jantar**	zhahn-TAR
special of the day	**prato do dia**	PRAH-too doo DEE-ah
specialty of the house	**especialidade da casa**	ish-peh-see-ah-lee-DAH-deh dah KAH-zah
tourist menu	**menu para turista**	MEH-noo PAH-rah too-REESH-tah
appetizers	**petiscos**	peh-TEESH-koosh
salad	**salada**	sah-LAH-dah
bread	**pão**	pow
soup	**sopa**	SOH-pah
first course	**primeira refeição**	pree-MAY-rah reh-fay-SOW
main course	**refeição principal**	reh-fay-SOW preen-see-PAHL
meat	**carne**	KAR-neh
poultry	**aves**	AH-vehsh
seafood	**marisco**	mah-REESH-koo
side dishes	**pratos á parte**	PRAH-toosh ah PAR-teh
vegetables	**legumes**	lay-GOO-mehsh
cheese	**queijo**	KAY-zhoo
dessert	**sobremesa**	soo-breh-MAY-zah
beverages	**bebidas**	beh-BEE-dahsh
beer	**cerveija**	sehr-VAY-zhah
wine	**vinho**	VEEN-yoo
service included	**serviço incluido**	sehr-VEE-soo een-kloo-EE-doo

service not included	**serviço não incluido**	sehr-VEE-soo now een-kloo-EE-doo
with / and / or / without	**com / e / ou / sem**	kohn / ee / oh / sayn

Restaurant requests and regrets:

A little.	**Um pouco.**	oon POH-koo
More.	**Mais.**	mīsh
Another.	**Outro.**	OH-troo
I did not order this.	**Não encomendei isto.**	now ayn-koo-mayn-DAY EESH-too
Is this included with the meal?	**Isto está incluido com a refeição?**	EESH-too ish-TAH een-kloo-EE-doo kohn ah reh-fay-SOW
What time does this open / close?	**A que horas é que abre / fecha?**	ah keh AW-rahsh eh keh AH-breh / FAY-shah
I'm in a hurry.	**Estou com pressa.**	ish-TOH kohn PREH-sah
When will the food be ready?	**Quando é que a comida vai estar pronta?**	KWAHN-doo eh keh ah koo-MEE-dah vī ish-TAR PROHN-tah
Can I get it "to go"?	**Posso levar o resto comigo?**	PAW-soo leh-VAR oo REHSH-too koo-MEE-goo
This is...	**Isto é...**	EESH-too eh
...dirty.	**...sujo.**	SOO-zhoo
...greasy.	**...gorduroso.**	gor-doo-ROH-zoo
...salty.	**...salgado.**	sahl-GAH-doo

...undercooked.	...malcozinhado.	mahl-koh-zeen-YAH-doo
...overcooked.	...queimado.	kay-MAH-doo
...inedible.	...não comestível.	now koh-mehsh-TEE-vehl
...cold.	...frio.	FREE-oo
Can you heat this up?	Pode aquecer a comida?	PAW-deh ah-kay-SEHR ah koo-MEE-dah
Yuk!	Porcaria!	poor-kah-REE-ah
Do your customers return?	Os seus clientes voltam outra vez?	oosh SEH-oosh klee-AYN-tehsh VOHL-tahm OH-trah vaysh
Enough.	Chega.	SHAY-gah
Finished.	Acabado.	ah-kah-BAH-doo
Delicious!	Delicioso!	deh-lee-see-OO-zoo
Very tasty!	Muito gostoso!	MWEEN-too goosh-TOH-zoo

Paying for your meal:

Waiter.	Criado.	kree-AH-doo
Waitress. (age 35+)	Senhora.	sin-YOH-rah
Waitress. (under 35)	Menina.	meh-NEE-nah
The bill, please.	A conta, por favor.	ah KOHN-tah poor fah-VOR
Together.	Conta junta.	KOHN-tah ZHOON-tah
Separate checks.	Conta separada.	KOHN-tah seh-pah-RAH-dah

Do you accept a credit card?	**Aceita cartão de crédito?**	ah-SAY-tah kar-TO<u>W</u> deh KRAY-dee-too
Is service included?	**O serviço está incluido?**	oo sehr-VEE-soo ish-TAH een-kloo-EE-doo
This is not correct.	**Isto não está certo.**	EESH-too no<u>w</u> ish-TAH SEHR-too
Can you explain this?	**Pode-me explicar isto?**	PAW-deh-meh ish-plee-KAR EESH-too
What if I wash the dishes?	**E se eu lavar os pratos?**	ee seh EH-oo lah-VAR oosh PRAH-toosh
Keep the change.	**Fique com o troco.**	FEE-keh koh<u>n</u> oo TROH-koo

On a Portuguese table:

table	**mesa**	MAY-zah
plate	**prato**	PRAH-too
napkin	**guardanapo**	gwar-dah-NAH-poo
knife	**faca**	FAH-kah
fork	**garfo**	GAR-foo
spoon	**colher**	KOOL-yehr
glass	**copo**	KAW-poo
carafe	**garrafa**	gah-RAH-fah
water	**água**	AH-gwah

Portuguese edible extras:

bread	**pão**	po<u>w</u>
butter	**manteiga**	mahn-TAY-gah
margarine	**margarina**	mar-gah-REE-nah

salt	**sal**	sahl
pepper	**pimenta**	pee-MAYN-tah
sugar	**açúcar**	ah-SOO-kar
artificial sweetener	**açúcar artificial**	ah-SOO-kar ar-tee-fee-see-AHL
honey	**mel**	mehl
mustard	**mostarda**	moosh-TAR-dah
mayonnaise	**maionese**	mah-yoh-NEH-zeh
olives	**azeitonas**	ah-ZAY-toh-nahs
pickles	**pepinos de conserva**	peh-PEE-noosh deh kohn-SEHR-vah
garlic	**alho**	AHL-yoo

What's for breakfast:

breakfast	**pequeno almoço**	peh-KAY-noo ahl-MOH-soo
eggs	**ovos**	AW-voosh
fried eggs	**ovos estrelados**	AW-voosh ish-treh-LAH-doosh
scrambled eggs	**ovos mexidos**	AW-voosh mish-EE-doosh
boiled egg...	**ovo cozido...**	AW-voo koo-ZEE-doo
...soft / hard	**...mole / duro**	MAW-leh / DOO-roo
omelet	**omeleta**	aw-meh-LEH-tah
ham	**presunto**	preh-ZOON-too
cheese	**queijo**	KAY-zhoo
bread	**pão**	pow
roll	**rolo**	ROH-loo
toast	**torrada**	toh-RAH-dah

jelly	**geláia**	zheh-LAY-ah
pastry	**pastelaria**	pahsh-teh-lah-REE-ah
yogurt	**yogurte**	yoo-GOOR-teh
cereal	**cereal**	seh-ree-AHL
milk	**leite**	LAY-teh
hot chocolate	**chocolate quente**	shoo-koo-LAH-teh KAYN-teh
fruit juice	**sumo de fruta**	SOO-moo deh FROO-tah
orange juice	**sumo de laranja**	SOO-moo deh lah-RAHN-zhah
coffee / tea (see Drinking)	**café / chá**	kah-FEH / shah
Is breakfast included (in the room cost)?	**O pequeno almoço está incluido?**	oo peh-KAY-noo ahl-MOH-soo ish-TAH een-kloo-EE-doo

Portuguese soups and salads:

soup	**sopa**	SOH-pah
broth...	**caldo...**	KAHL-doo
...chicken	**...frango**	FRANG-goo
...meat	**...carne**	KAR-neh
...with noodles	**...com massa**	kohn MAH-sah
...with rice	**...com arroz**	kohn ah-ROHSH
shellfish soup	**açorda de marisco**	ah-SOR-dah deh mah-REESH-koo
potato and cabbage soup	**caldo verde**	KAHL-doo VEHR-deh

thick vegetable soup	**sopa de legumes**	SOH-pah deh lay-GOO-mehsh
green salad	**salada de alface**	sah-LAH-dah deh ahl-FAH-seh
mixed salad	**salada mista**	sah-LAH-dah MEESH-tah
octopus salad	**salada de polvo**	sah-LAH-dah deh POHL-voo
lettuce	**alface**	ahl-FAH-seh
tomatoes	**tomates**	too-MAH-tehsh
cucumbers	**pepinos**	peh-PEE-noosh
oil / vinegar	**óleo / vinagre**	AWL-yoo / vee-NAH-greh
What is in this salad?	**O que é isto na salada?**	oo keh eh EESH-too nah sah-LAH-dah

Portuguese seafood:

seafood	**marisco**	mah-REESH-koo
assorted seafood	**diversos mariscos**	dee-VEHR-soosh mah-REESH-koosh
fish	**peixe**	PAY-sheh
cod	**bacalhau**	bah-kahl-YOW
salmon	**salmão**	sahl-MOW
trout	**truta**	TROO-tah
tuna	**atum**	ah-TOOM
herring	**arenque**	ah-RAYN-keh
sardines	**sardinhas**	sar-DEEN-yahsh
anchovies	**anchovas**	ahn-SHOH-vahsh

clams	**amêijoas**	ah-MAY-zhoo-ahsh
mussels	**mexilhões**	meh-sheel-YOHNSH
oysters	**ostras**	OHSH-trahsh
shrimp	**camarão**	kah-mah-RO<u>W</u>
prawns	**gambas**	GAHM-bahsh
crab	**carangueijo**	kah-rahn-GAY-zhoo
lobster	**lagosta**	lah-GOHSH-tah
octopus	**polvo**	POHL-voo
squid	**lulas**	LOO-lahsh
Here's looking	**Está a olhar**	ish-TAH ah ohl-YAR
at you, squid!	**para ti, lulas!**	PAH-rah tee LOO-lahsh

Portuguese poultry and meat:

poultry	**aves**	AH-vehsh
chicken	**frango**	FRANG-goo
stewing chicken	**galinha**	gah-LEEN-yah
turkey	**peru**	peh-ROO
duck	**pato**	PAH-too
meat	**carne**	KAR-neh
beef	**carne de vaca**	KAR-neh deh VAH-kah
roast beef	**carne assada**	KAR-neh ah-SAH-dah
beef steak	**bife**	BEE-feh
ribsteak	**costelas**	kohsh-TEH-lahsh
veal	**vitela**	vee-TEH-lah
cutlet	**costeleta**	koosh-teh-LAY-tah
pork	**porco**	POR-koo
ham	**presunto**	preh-ZOON-too
lamb	**carneiro**	kar-NAY-roo

bunny	**coelho**	KWAYL-yoo
snails	**caracóis**	kah-rah-KOYSH
brains	**miolos**	mee-OH-loosh
tongue	**lingua**	LEENG-gwah
liver	**fígado**	FEE-gah-doo
tripe	**tripas**	TREE-pahsh
How long has this been dead?	**À quanto tempo é que isto está morto?**	ah KWAHN-too TAYN-poo eh keh EESH-too ish-TAH MOR-too

How it's prepared in Portugal:

hot	**quente**	KAYN-teh
cold	**frio**	FREE-oo
raw	**crú**	kroo
cooked	**cozido**	koo-ZEE-doo
baked	**no forno**	noo FOR-noo
boiled	**ferver**	fehr-VEHR
fillet	**filé**	fee-LEH
fresh	**fresco**	FRAYSH-koo
fried	**frito**	FREE-too
grilled	**grilhado**	greel-YAH-doo
microwave	**micro ondas**	MEE-kroo OHN-dahsh
mild	**médio**	MEH-dee-oo
poached	**escalfado**	ish-kahl-FAH-doo
roasted	**assado**	ah-SAH-doo
smoked	**fumado**	foo-MAH-doo
spicy hot	**picante**	pee-KAHN-teh
steamed	**cozido ao vapor**	koo-ZEE-doo ow vah-POR

stuffed	**recheio**	reh-SHAY-oo
rare	**mal passado**	mahl pah-SAH-doo
medium	**meio passado**	MAY-oo pah-SAH-doo
well-done	**bem passado**	bayn pah-SAH-doo

Portuguese veggies, pasta and rice:

vegetables	**legumes**	lay-GOO-mehsh
artichoke	**alcachofra**	ahl-kah-SHAW-frah
asparagus	**espargos**	ish-PAR-goosh
beans	**feijões**	fay-ZHOHNSH
beets	**beterraba**	beh-teh-RAH-bah
broccoli	**brócolos**	BRAW-koo-loosh
cabbage	**couve**	KOH-veh
carrots	**cenoura**	seh-NOH-rah
cauliflower	**couve-flor**	KOH-veh-flor
corn	**milho**	MEEL-yoo
eggplant	**berinjela**	beh-reen-ZHEH-lah
green beans	**feijões verdes**	fay-ZHOHNSH VEHR-dehsh
green peppers	**pimentos verdes**	pee-MAYN-toosh VEHR-dehsh
mushrooms	**cogumelos**	koo-goo-MEH-loosh
onions	**cebolas**	seh-BOH-lahsh
peas	**ervilhas**	ehr-VEEL-yahsh
spinach	**espinafre**	ish-peen-NAH-freh
zucchini	**zukini**	zoo-KEE-nee
potato	**batata**	bah-TAH-tah

French fries	**batatas fritas**	bah-TAH-tahsh FREE-tahsh
pasta	**massa**	MAH-sah
spaghetti	**esparguete**	ish-par-GEH-teh
rice	**arroz**	ah-ROHSH

Portuguese specialties to watch for:

caldo verde	potato and cabbage soup
caracóis	snails (summer only)
chouriços	smoked pork sausage
bacalhau	cod (prepared a thousand different ways)
bolinhos de bacalhau	codfish balls
caldeirada	fish stew
coelho à caçador	rabbit, hunter's style (with carrots and potatoes)
costeletas de porco à alentejana	pork chops, Alentejo-style (with tomatoes and onions)
cozido à portuguesa	meats, vegetables, and rice
feijoada	beans with pork and sausage
leitão	small roasted pig
perna de cabrito	roasted leg of baby goat

Portuguese fruit:

fruit	**fruta**	FROO-tah
apple	**maçã**	mah-SAH
apricot	**damasco**	dah-MAHSH-koo
banana	**banana**	bah-NAH-nah
cherry	**cereja**	seh-RAY-zhah
coconut	**coco**	KOH-koo
date	**fruto seco**	FROO-too SAY-koo
fig	**figo**	FEE-goo
grapefruit	**toranja**	too-RAHN-zhah
grapes	**uvas**	OO-vahsh
lemon	**limão**	lee-MO<u>W</u>
melon	**melão**	meh-LO<u>W</u>
orange	**laranja**	lah-RAHN-zhah
peach	**pêssago**	PAY-sah-goo
pear	**pêra**	PAY-rah
pineapple	**ananás**	ah-nah-NAHSH
plum	**ameixa**	ah-MAY-shah
prune	**ameixa seca**	ah-MAY-shah SAY-kah
raspberry	**framboesa**	frahm-boo-AY-zah
strawberry	**morango**	moo-RANG-goo
tangerine	**tangerina**	tahn-zheh-REE-nah
watermelon	**melancia**	meh-LAHN-see-ah

Nuts to you:

almond	**amêndoa**	ah-MAYN-doh-ah
chestnut	**castanha**	kahsh-TAHN-yah
hazelnut	**avelã**	ah-veh-LAH
peanut	**amendoim**	ah-mayn-DWEEM
pistachio	**pistácio**	peesh-TAH-see-oo
walnut	**noz**	nawsh

Portuguese desserts and goodies:

dessert	**sobremesa**	soo-breh-MAY-zah
flan	**flan**	flahn
cake	**bolo**	BOH-loo
ice cream	**gelado**	zheh-LAH-doo
fruit cup	**taça de fruta**	TAH-sah deh FROO-tah
tart	**tarte**	TAR-teh
whipped cream	**chântily**	SHAHN-tee-lee
mousse	**mousse**	MOO-seh
caramel custard	**pudim**	POO-deem
pastry	**pastelaria**	pahsh-teh-lah-REE-ah
cookies	**bolos**	BOH-loosh
candy	**rebuçados**	ray-boo-SAH-doosh
low calorie	**poucas calorias**	POH-kahsh kah-loo-REE-ahsh
homemade	**caseiro**	kah-ZAY-roo
Exquisite!	**Requintado!**	ray-keen-TAH-doo
It's heavenly!	**É divinal!**	eh dee-vee-NAHL

Drinking

Portuguese water, milk, and juice:

mineral water	**água mineral**	AH-gwah mee-neh-RAHL
tap water	**água da torneira**	AH-gwah dah tor-NAY-rah
whole milk	**leite gordo**	LAY-teh GOR-doo
skim milk	**leite magro**	LAY-teh MAH-groo
fresh milk	**leite fresco**	LAY-teh FRAYSH-koo
hot chocolate	**chocolate quente**	shoo-koo-LAH-teh KAYN-teh
fruit juice (pure)	**sumo de fruta (puro)**	SOO-moo deh FROO-tah (POO-roo)
orange juice	**sumo de laranja**	SOO-moo deh lah-RAHN-zhah
with / without...	**com / sem...**	kohn / sayn
...carbonation	**...gás**	gahsh
...sugar	**...açúcar**	ah-SOO-kar
...ice	**...gelo**	ZHAY-loo
glass / cup	**copo / chávena**	KAW-poo / SHAH-veh-nah
small / large	**pequena / grande**	peh-KAY-nah / GRAHN-deh
bottle	**garrafa**	gah-RAH-fah
Is this water safe to drink?	**Posso beber esta água?**	PAW-soo beh-BEHR EHSH-tah AH-gwah

Tap water is free at restaurants, but you have to ask for it. If you like mineral water, *Água do Luso* is a popular brand without carbonation. *Água das Pedras* is a brand with carbonation. The light, sturdy plastic water bottles are great to pack along and re-use as you travel.

Portuguese coffee and tea:

coffee...	**café...**	kah-FEH
...with milk	**...com leite**	kohn LAY-teh
...with sugar	**...com açucar**	kohn ah-SOO-kar
...decaffeinated	**...descaféenado**	dish-kah-feh-NAH-doo
...instant	**...instantaneo**	eensh-tahn-TAHN-yoo
espresso	**bica**	BEE-kah
espresso with milk	**garoto**	gah-ROH-too
hot water	**água quente**	AH-gwah KAYN-teh
tea / lemon	**chá / limão**	shah / lee-MOW
herbal tea	**chá de ervas**	shah deh EHR-vahsh
iced tea	**chá gelado**	shah zheh-LAH-doo
small / large	**pequeno / grande**	peh-KAY-noo / GRAHN-deh
Another cup.	**Outra chávena.**	OH-trah SHAH-veh-nah

Portuguese wine:

wine	**vinho**	VEEN-yoo
table wine	**vinho de mesa**	VEEN-yoo deh MAY-zah
cheap house wine	**vinho da casa**	VEEN-yoo dah KAH-zah
local	**local**	loo-KAHL
red	**tinto**	TEEN-too
white	**branco**	BRANG-koo
rose	**rosé**	roh-ZEH
sparkling	**espumante**	ish-poo-MAHN-teh
sweet	**doce**	DOH-seh
medium	**médio**	MEH-dee-oo
dry	**seco**	SAY-koo
very dry	**muito seco**	MWEEN-too SAY-koo
A glass...	**Um copo...**	oo<u>n</u> KAW-poo
A bottle...	**Uma garrafa...**	OO-mah gah-RAH-fah
...of red wine.	**...de vinho tinto.**	deh VEEN-yoo TEEN-too
...of white wine.	**...de vinho branco.**	deh VEEN-yoo BRANG-koo
The wine list.	**A lista de vinhos.**	ah LEESH-tah deh VEEN-yoosh

For good, cheap wine, try the *vinho de casa*. A Portuguese specialty is *vinho verde*, a sparkling wine which comes in red or white--while many argue that both are bad, the white is clearly better.

Portuguese beer:

beer	**cerveja**	sehr-VAY-zhah
glass of draft beer	**fino**	FEE-noo
big glass of draft beer	**caneca**	kah-NEH-kah
bottle	**garrafa**	gah-RAH-fah
small / large	**pequena / grande**	peh-KAY-nah / GRAHN-deh
local / imported	**local / importada**	loo-KAHL / eem-poor-TAH-dah
cold	**fresca**	FREHSH-kah
colder	**gelada**	zheh-LAH-dah

Portuguese bar talk:

local specialty	**especialidade local**	ish-peh-see-ah-lee-DAH-deh loo-KAHL
straight	**puro**	POO-roo
with / without ice	**com / sem gelo**	kohn / sayn ZHAY-loo
One more.	**Mais uma.**	mīsh OO-mah
Cheers!	**Saúde!**	sah-OO-deh
Long live Portugal!	**Vida longa Portugal!**	VEE-dah LOHN-gah poor-too-GAHL
I'm feeling a little drunk.	**Estou-me a sentir um bocado bêbado[a].**	ish-TOH-meh ah sayn-TEER oon boo-KAH-doo BAY-bah-doo

Groceries and Picnics

Portuguese picnic words:

open air market	**mercado municipal**	mehr-KAH-doo moo-nee-see-PAHL
grocery store	**mercearia**	mehr-see-ah-REE-ah
supermarket	**supermercado**	soo-pehr-mehr-KAH-doo
picnic	**piquenique**	peek-NEEK
sandwich	**sande, sanduíche**	SAHN-deh, sahnd-WEE-sheh
bread (whole wheat)	**pão (de trigo)**	POW (deh TREE-goo)
roll	**rolo**	ROH-loo
meat and egg roll	**prego no pão**	PRAY-goo noo pow
toasted cheese and ham sandwich	**tosta mista**	TOHSH-tah MEESH-tah
ham	**presunto**	preh-ZOON-too
sausage	**salsicha**	sahl-SEE-shah
cheese	**queijo**	KAY-zhoo
yogurt	**yogurte**	yoo-GOOR-teh
plastic spoon	**colher plástica**	KOOL-yehr PLAHSH-tee-koo
plastic cup	**copo plástico**	KAW-poo PLAHSH-tee-koo
paper plate	**prato de papel**	PRAH-too deh pah-PEHL

At the Portuguese grocery:

Is it self-service?	**É self-service?**	eh "self-service"
May I taste a little?	**Posso provar um bocadinho?**	PAW-soo proo-VAR oon boo-kah-DEEN-yoo
Fifty grams.	**Cinquenta gramas.**	seeng-KWAYN-tah GRAH-mahsh
One hundred grams.	**Cem gramas.**	sayn GRAH-mahsh
More. / Less.	**Mais. / Menos.**	mīsh / MAY-noosh
A piece.	**Um pedaço.**	oon peh-DAH-soo
A slice.	**Uma fatia.**	OO-mah fah-TEE-ah
Sliced.	**Ás fatias.**	ahsh fah-TEE-ahsh
Will you make me a sandwich?	**Pode-me fazer uma sande?**	PAW-deh-meh fah-ZEHR OO-mah SAHN-deh
To take out.	**Levar para fora.**	leh-VAR PAH-rah FOR-rah
Is there a park nearby?	**Há algum parque perto?**	ah AHL-goom PAR-keh PEHR-too
May we picnic here?	**Podemos fazer um piquenique aqui?**	poh-DAY-moosh fah-ZEHR oon peek-NEEK ah-KEE
Enjoy your meal!	**Bom-apetite!**	bohm-ah-peh-TEE-teh

You can shop for your picnic at a one-stop *supermercado*, but it's more fun to practice your Portuguese while visiting the small shops. You can get bread for your sandwiches at a *padaria* and order meat and cheese by the gram at a *mercearia*.

Sightseeing

Handy Portuguese sightseeing questions:

Where is...? / Where are...?	**Onde é...? / Onde estão...?**	OHN-deh eh / OHN-deh ish-TOW
...the best view	**...a melhor vista**	ah mil-YOR VEESH-tah
...the main square	**...a praça principal**	ah PRAH-sah preen-see-PAHL
...the old town center	**...a parte da cidade velha**	ah PAR-teh dah see-DAH-deh VEHL-yah
...the town hall	**...a câmara da cidade**	ah KAH-mah-rah dah see-DAH-dah
...the museum	**...o museu**	oo moo-ZEH-oo
...the castle	**...o castelo**	oo kahsh-TEH-loo
...the ruins	**...as ruínas**	ahsh roo-EE-nahsh
...a festival	**...o festival**	oo fehsh-tee-VAHL
...a fair	**...a feira**	ah FAY-rah
...tourist information	**...a informação turistica**	ah een-for-mah-SOW too-REESH-tee-kah
Do you have... in English?	**Tem... em inglês?**	tayn... ayn een-GLAYSH
...information	**...informações**	een-for-mah-SOHNSH
...a guidebook	**...um guia**	oon GEE-ah
...a tour	**...uma excursão**	OO-mah ish-koor-SOW
When is the next tour...?	**Quando é a próxima excursão...?**	KWAHN-doo eh ah PRAW-see-mah ish-koor-SOW

...in English	...em inglês	ayn een-GLAYSH
Is it free?	Isto é grátis?	EESH-too eh GRAH-teesh
How much does it cost?	Quanto custa?	KWAHN-too KOOSH-tah
Is there a discount for...?	Tem desconto para...?	tayn dish-KOHN-too PAH-rah
...students	...estudantes	ish-too-DAHN-tehsh
...seniors	...pessoas de terceira idade	peh-SOH-ahsh deh tehr-SAY-rah ee-DAH-deh
...youth	...jovens	ZHAW-vahnsh
Is the ticket good all day?	O bilhete é bom para o dia inteiro?	oo beel-YEH-teh eh bohn PAH-rah oo DEE-ah een-TAY-roo
What time does this open / close?	A que horas é que abre / fecha?	ah keh AW-rahsh eh keh AH-breh / FAY-shah
What time is the last entry?	A que horas é a última entrada?	ah keh AW-rahsh eh ah OOL-tee-mah ayn-TRAH-dah
PLEASE let me in.	POR FAVOR deixe-me entrar.	poor fah-VOR DAY-sheh-meh ayn-TRAR
I've traveled all the way from...	Estou a viajar de muito longe...	ish-TOH ah vee-ah-ZHAR deh MWEEN-too LOHN-zheh
I must leave tomorrow.	Tenho que partir amanhã.	TAYN-yoo keh par-TEER ah-ming-YAH

In the museum:

Where can I find this? (point to photo)	**Onde é que posso encontrar isto?**	OHN-deh eh keh PAW-soo ayn-kohn-TRAR EESH-too
I'd like to see...	**Gostaria de ver...**	goosh-tah-REE-ah deh vehr
Can I...?	**Posso...?**	PAW-soo
...take photos	**...tirar fotografias**	tee-RAR foo-too-grah-FEE-ahsh
...use a video camera	**...utilizar a câmara vídeo**	oo-tee-lee-ZAR ah KAH-mah-rah VEE-day-oo
No flash / tripod.	**Não flash / tripé.**	now flahsh / tree-PEH
I like it.	**Gosto desta.**	GAWSH-too DEHSH-tah
It's so...	**É tão...**	eh tow
...beautiful.	**...lindo.**	LEEN-doo
...ugly.	**...feio.**	FAY-oo
...strange.	**...estranho.**	ish-TRAHN-yoo
...boring.	**...enfadonho.**	ayn-fah-DOHN-yoo
...interesting.	**...interessante.**	een-teh-reh-SAHN-teh
Wow!	**Fiche!**	FEE-sheh
My feet hurt!	**Os meus pés estão cansados!**	oosh MEH-oosh pehsh ish-TOW kahn-SAH-doosh
I'm exhausted!	**Estou estoirado!**	ish-TOH ish-toy-RAH-doo

Art and architecture:

English	Portuguese	Pronunciation
art	**arte**	AR-teh
artist	**artista**	ar-TEESH-tah
painting	**pintura**	peen-TOO-rah
self portrait	**auto-retrato**	ow-too-reh-TRAH-too
sculptor	**escultor**	ish-kool-TOR
sculpture	**escultura**	ish-kool-TOO-rah
architect	**arquiteto**	ar-kee-TEH-too
architecture	**arquitetura**	ar-kee-teh-TOO-rah
original	**original**	oo-ree-zhee-NAHL
restored	**restaurado**	rish-too-RAH-doo
B.C.	**A.C.**	ahn-tehsh deh KREESH-too
A.D.	**D.C.**	deh-POYSH deh KREESH-too
century	**secúlo**	seh-KOO-loo
style	**estilo**	ish-TEE-loo
Abstract	**abstracto**	ahbsh-TRAH-too
Ancient	**antigo**	ahn-TEE-goo
Art Nouveau	**arte nova**	AR-teh NOH-vah
Baroque	**barroco**	bah-ROH-koo
Classical	**clássico**	KLAH-see-koo
Gothic	**gótico**	GAW-tee-koo
Impressionist	**impressionista**	eem-preh-see-oo-NEESH-tah
Medieval	**mediaval**	meh-dee-ah-VAHL
Moorish	**mouro**	MOH-roo

Renaissance	**renascimento**	reh-nahsh-see-MAYN-too
Romanesque	**românico**	roo-MAH-nee-koo
Romantic	**romântico**	roo-MAHN-tee-koo

Portugal's golden age of trade and exploration gave birth to a lavish, flamboyant Gothic style called "Manueline," named after King Manuel of the early 16th century.

Castles and palaces:

castle	**castelo**	kahs-TEH-loo
palace	**palâcio**	pah-LAH-see-oo
ballroom	**salão de festas**	sah-LOW deh FEHSH-tahsh
kitchen	**cozinha**	koo-ZEEN-yah
cellar	**celeiro**	seh-LAY-roo
dungeon	**masmorra**	mahsh-MOH-rah
fortified walls	**fortificação**	for-tee-fee-kah-KOW
tower	**torre**	TOR-reh
fountain	**fonte**	FOHN-teh
garden	**jardim**	zhar-DEEM
king	**rei**	ray
queen	**raínha**	rah-EEN-yah
knights	**cavaleiros**	kah-vah-LAY-roosh

Portuguese religious words:

cathedral	**catedral**	kah-teh-DRAHL
church	**igreija**	ee-GRAY-zhah
monastery	**monestério**	moo-nehsh-TEH-ree-oo
mosque	**mesquita**	mehsh-KEE-tah
synagogue	**sinagoga**	see-nah-GOH-gah
chapel	**capela**	kah-PEH-lah
altar	**altar**	ahl-TAR
cross	**cruz**	kroosh
crypt	**caixão**	kī-SHOW
dome	**cúpula**	KOO-poo-lah
organ	**orgão**	or-GOW
relic	**rélica**	REH-lee-kah
saint	**santo[a]**	SAHN-too
God	**Deus**	DEH-oosh
Jewish	**Judeu**	ZHOO-deh-oo
Muslim	**Muçulmano**	moo-sool-MAH-noo
Christian	**Cristão**	kreesh-TOW
Protestant	**Prostetante**	proosh-teh-TAYN-teh
Catholic	**Católico**	kah-TAW-lee-koo
When is the mass / service?	**Quando é que é a missa / serviço?**	KWAHN-doo eh keh eh ah MEE-sah / sehr-VEE-soo
Are there concerts in the church?	**Dão concertos na igreja?**	dow kohn-SEHR-toosh nah ee-GRAY-zhah

Shopping

Names of Portuguese shops:

antiques	**antiquário**	ahn-tee-KWAH-ree-oo
art gallery	**galeria de arte**	gah-leh-REE-ah deh AR-teh
bakery	**padaria**	pah-dah-REE-ah
barber shop	**barbeiro**	bar-BAY-roo
beauty parlor	**cabelareiro**	kah-beh-lah-RAY-roo
book shop	**livraria**	leev-rah-REE-ah
camera shop	**loja fotográfica**	LAW-zhah foo-too-GRAH-fee-kah
department store	**grande armazen**	GRAHN-deh ar-mah-ZAYN
flea market	**feira**	FAY-rah
flower market	**mercado de flores**	mehr-KAH-doo deh FLOH-rehs
grocery store	**mercearia**	mehr-see-ah-REE-ah
jewelry shop	**joalheria**	zhoo-ahl-yeh-REE-ah
laundromat	**lavandaria**	lah-vahn-dah-REE-ah
newsstand	**quiosque**	kee-AWSH-keh
open air market	**mercado municipal**	mehr-KAH-doo moo-nee-see-PAHL
pharmacy	**farmácia**	far-MAH-see-ah
shopping mall	**centro comercial**	SAYN-troo koo-mehr-see-AHL

souvenir shop	**loja de lembranças**	LAW-zhah deh laym-BRANG-sahsh
supermarket	**supermercado**	soo-pehr-mehr-KAH-doo
toy store	**loja de brinquedos**	LAW-zhah deh breen-KAY-doosh
travel agency	**agência de viagens**	ah-ZHAYN-see-ah deh vee-AH-zhay<u>n</u>sh
used bookstore	**loja de livros usados**	LAW-zhah deh LEEV-roosh oo-ZAH-doosh
wine shop	**loja de vinhos**	LAW-zhah deh VEEN-yoosh

In Portugal, most shops close for lunch from about 13:00 till 15:00 and all day on Sundays.

Shop till you drop:

sale	**saldo**	SAHL-doo
How much does it cost?	**Quanto custa?**	KWAHN-too KOOSH-tah
I'd like...	**Gostaria...**	goosh-tah-REE-ah
Do you have...?	**Tem...?**	tay<u>n</u>
...something cheaper	**...alguma coisa mais barato**	ahl-GOO-mah KOY-zah mīsh bah-RAH-too
...more	**...mais**	mīsh
Can I see...?	**Posso ver...?**	PAW-soo vehr
This one.	**Este aqui.**	AYSH-teh ah-KEE

Can I try it on?	**Posso exprimentar?**	PAW-soo ish-pree-mayn-TAR
Do you have a mirror?	**Tem um espelho?**	tay<u>n</u> <u>oo</u>n ish-PAYL-yoo
It's too...	**É muito...**	eh MWEEN-too
...big.	**...grande.**	GRAHN-deh
...small.	**...pequeno.**	peh-KAY-noo
...expensive.	**...caro.**	KAH-roo
Did you make this?	**Foi você que fez isto?**	foy voh-SAY keh fehsh EESH-too
What is this made of?	**Isto é feito de quê?**	EESH-too eh FAY-too deh kay
Is it machine washable?	**Posso lavar á máquina?**	PAW-soo lah-VAR ah MAH-kee-nah
Will it shrink?	**Vai encolher?**	vī ayn-kohl-YEHR
Can you ship this?	**Pode enviar isto?**	PAW-deh ayn-vee-AR EESH-too
Do you accept a credit card?	**Aceita cartão de crédito?**	ah-SAY-tah kar-TO<u>W</u> deh KRAY-dee-too
Tax-free?	**Livre de impostos?**	LEE-vreh deh eem-POHSH-toosh
I'll think about it.	**Vou pensar.**	voh payn-SAR
What time do you close?	**A que horas é que fecha?**	ah keh AW-rahsh eh keh FAY-shah
What time do you open tomorrow?	**A que horas é que abre amanhã?**	ah keh AW-rahsh eh keh AH-breh ah-ming-YAH
Is that your best price?	**É o seu melhor preço?**	eh oo SEH-oo mil-YOR PRAY-soo

My last offer.	**A minha última oferta.**	ah MEEN-yah OOL-tee-mah oo-FEHR-tah
I'm nearly broke.	**Estou quase sem dinheiro.**	ish-TOH KWAH-zeh sayn deen-YAY-roo
I'm... / We're...	**Estou... / Estamos...**	ish-TOH / ish-TAH-moosh
...browsing.	**...só a olhar.**	saw ah ohl-YAR
My male friend...	**O meu amigo...**	oo MEH-oo ah-MEE-goo
My female friend...	**A minha amiga...**	ah MEEN-yah ah-MEE-gah
My husband...	**O meu marido...**	oo MEH-oo mah-REE-doo
My wife...	**A minha mulher...**	ah MEEN-yah MOOL-yehr
...has the money.	**...é que tem o dinheiro.**	eh keh tayn oo deen-YAY-roo

Mail

Licking the Portuguese postal code:

post office	**correios**	koo-RAY-oosh
stamp	**selo**	SAY-loo
post card	**cartão postal**	kar-TOW poosh-TAHL
letter	**carta**	KAR-tah
aerogram	**telegrama aéreo**	teh-leh-GRAH-mah
		ah-EH-ray-oh
envelope	**envelope**	ayn-veh-LOH-peh
package	**enbalagem**	ayn-bah-LAH-zhayn
box	**caixa**	KĪ-shah
string	**cordão**	kor-DOW
tape	**adesivo**	ah-deh-ZEE-voo
mailbox	**caixa postal**	KĪ-shah poosh-TAHL
air mail	**correio aéreo**	koo-RAY-oo
		ah-EH-ray-oo
express	**expresso**	ish-PREH-soo
surface mail	**terrestre**	teh-REHSH-treh
(slow and cheap)		
book rate	**á tabela**	ah tah-BEH-lah
	do livro	doo LEE-vroo
registered	**registrado**	ray-zheesh-TRAH-doo
insured	**seguro**	say-GOO-roo
fragile	**frágil**	FRAH-zheel
contents	**conteúdo**	kohn-teh-OO-doo

customs	**alfândega**	ahl-FAHN-deh-gah
to / from	**para / de**	PAH-rah / deh
address	**endereço**	ayn-deh-RAY-soo
zip code	**código postal**	KAW-dee-goo poosh-TAHL
general delivery	**Posta Restante**	PAWSH-tah rish-TAHN-teh

Mail bonding:

Where is the post office?	**Onde é que é os correios?**	OHN-deh eh keh eh oosh koo-RAY-oosh
Which window for...?	**Que janela para...?**	keh zhah-NEH-lah PAH-rah
To the United States.	**Para os Estados Unidos.**	PAH-rah oosh ish-TAH-doosh oo-NEE-doosh
How much does it cost?	**Quanto custa?**	KWAHN-too KOOSH-tah
How many days...?	**Quantos dias...?**	KWAHN-toosh DEE-ahsh
How many weeks...?	**Quantas semanas...?**	KWAHN-tahsh seh-MAHN-ahsh
How many months...?	**Quantos meses...?**	KWAHN-toosh MAY-zehsh
...will it take	**...é que demora**	eh keh deh-MOH-rah

In Portugal, you can often get stamps at a newsstand (*quiosque*) or a tobacco shop (*tabacaria*).

Time

Portuguese time:

What time is it?	**Que horas são?**	keh AW-rahsh so<u>w</u>
It's...	**São...**	so<u>w</u>
...8:00 in the morning.	**...oito horas da manhã.**	OY-too AW-rahsh dah ming-NYAH
...16:00.	**...dezasseis horas.**	deh-zah-SAYSH AW-rahsh
...9:30 in the evening.	**...nove horas e meia da noite.**	NAW-veh AW-rahsh ee MAY-ah dah NOY-teh
...a quarter past three.	**...quinze minutos depois das três.**	KEEN-zeh mee-NOO-toosh deh-POYSH dahsh traysh
...a quarter to eleven.	**...um quarto para as onze.**	oo<u>n</u> KWAR-too PAH-rah ahs OHN-zeh
...about 4:00 in the afternoon.	**...cerca das quarto da tarde.**	SEHR-kah dahsh KWAR-too dah TAR-deh
...noon.	**...meio-dia.**	may-oo-DEE-ah
...midnight.	**...meia-noite.**	may-ah-NOY-teh
...too early.	**...muito cedo.**	MWEEN-too SAY-doo
...too late.	**...muito tarde.**	MWEEN-too TAR-deh

Timely words:

minute	**minuto**	mee-NOO-too
hour	**hora**	AW-rah
in one hour	**em uma hora**	ayn OO-mah AW-rah
immediately	**imediatamente**	ee-meh-dee-ah-tah-MAYN-teh
any time	**a qualquer hora**	ah kwahl-KEHR AW-rah
every hour	**todas as horas**	TOH-dahs ahsh AW-rahsh
every day	**todos os dias**	TOH-doosh oosh DEE-ahsh
May 15	**quinze de Maio**	KEEN-zeh deh MAH-yoo
in the morning	**da manhã**	dah ming-YAH
in the afternoon	**da tarde**	dah TAR-deh
in the evening	**da noite**	dah NOY-teh
night	**noite**	NOY-teh
day	**dia**	DEE-ah
today	**hoje**	OH-zheh
yesterday	**ontem**	OHN-tayn
tomorrow	**amanhã**	ah-ming-YAH
tomorrow morning	**amanhã de manhã**	ah-ming-YAH deh ming-YAH
week	**semana**	seh-MAH-nah
month	**mês**	maysh
year	**ano**	AH-noo

last	**último**	OOL-tee-moo
this	**este**	AYSH-teh
next	**próximo**	PRAW-see-moo
Monday	**segunda-feira**	seh-goon-dah-FAY-rah
Tuesday	**terça-feira**	tehr-sah-FAY-rah
Wednesday	**quarta-feira**	kwar-tah-FAY-rah
Thursday	**quinta-feira**	keen-tah-FAY-rah
Friday	**sexta-feira**	saysh-tah-FAY-rah
Saturday	**sábado**	SAH-bah-doo
Sunday	**domingo**	doo-MEENG-goo
January	**Janeiro**	zhah-NAY-roo
February	**Fevereiro**	feh-veh-RAY-roo
March	**Março**	MAR-soo
April	**Abril**	ah-BREEL
May	**Maio**	MAH-yoo
June	**Junho**	ZHOON-yoo
July	**Julho**	ZHOOL-yoo
August	**Agosto**	ah-GOHSH-too
September	**Setembro**	seh-TAYN-broo
October	**Outubro**	oh-TOO-broo
November	**Novembro**	noo-VAYN-broo
December	**Dezembro**	deh-ZAYN-broo
spring	**primavera**	pree-mah-VEH-rah
summer	**verão**	veh-ROW
fall	**outono**	oh-TOH-noo
winter	**inverno**	een-VEHR-noo

Happy holidays:

holiday	**feriado**	feh-ree-AH-doo
national holiday	**feriado nacional**	feh-ree-AH-doo nah-see-oo-NAHL
religious holiday	**feriado religioso**	feh-ree-AH-doo ray-lee-zhee-OH-zoo
Happy birthday!	**Feliz aniversário!**	feh-LEESH ah-nee-vehr-SAH-ree-oo
Happy wedding anniversary!	**Feliz aniversário de casamento!**	feh-LEESH ah-nee-vehr-SAH-ree-oo deh kah-zah-MAYN-too
Merry Christmas!	**Feliz Natal!**	feh-LEESH nah-TAHL
Happy New Year!	**Feliz Ano Novo!**	feh-LEESH AH-noo NOH-voo

Portugal celebrates its independence day on September 7th. Other major holidays include Easter week, *Dia de Camões* (June 10th, in honor of the Portuguese poet Luis de Camões), *Ascenção de Maria* (August 15th), and *Dia da República* (October 5th).

Red Tape and Profanity

Filling out Portuguese forms:

Sr. / Sra. / Menina	Mr. / Mrs. / Miss
nome	first name
apelido	last name
endereço	address
rua	street
cidade	city
estado	state
pais	country
nacionalidade	nationality
origem / destino	origin / destination
idade	age
dia de nascimento	date of birth
lugar de nascimento	place of birth
sexo	sex
masculino	male
feminino	female
casado / casada	married man / married woman
solteiro / solteira	single man / single woman
profissão	profession
adulto	adult
criança / rapaz / rapariga	child / boy / girl
crianças	children
familia	family
assinatura	signature
data	date

Portuguese profanity:

Go to hell!	**Vá para o inferno!**	vah PAH-rah oo een-FEHR-noo
Damn it!	**Maldito seja!**	mahl-DEE-too SAY-zhah
bastard	**bastardo**	bahsh-TAR-doo
bitch	**puta**	POO-tah
breasts (colloq.)	**mamas**	MAH-mahsh
penis (colloq.)	**caralho**	kah-RAHL-yoo
shit	**merda**	MEHR-dah
drunk	**bêbado**	BAY-bah-doo
idiot	**idiota**	ee-dee-OH-tah
imbecile	**tolo[a]**	TOH-loo
jerk	**palermo[a]**	pah-LEHR-moo
stupid	**estúpido[a]**	ish-TOO-pee-doo
cretin	**cretino**	kreh-TEE-noo
Did someone...?	**Alguem deu...?**	AHL-gayn DEH-oo
...fart	**...um peido**	oon PAY-doo
...burp	**...um arroto**	oon ah-ROH-too

Health

Handy Portuguese health words:

pain	**dor**	dor
dentist	**dentista**	dayn-TEESH-tah
doctor	**doutor[a]**	doh-TOR
nurse	**enfermeira**	ayn-fehr-MAY-rah
health insurance	**seguro de saúde**	say-GOO-roo deh sah-OO-deh
hospital	**hospital**	ohsh-pee-TAHL
medicine	**medicina**	meh-dee-ZEE-nah
pharmacy	**farmácia**	far-MAH-see-ah
prescription	**receita**	reh-SAY-tah
pill	**comprimido**	kohm-pree-MEE-doo
aspirin	**aspirina**	ahsh-pee-REE-nah
antibiotic	**antibiótico**	ahn-tee-bee-AW-tee-koo
pain killer	**comprimidos para as dores**	kohm-pree-MEE-doosh PAH-rah ahsh DOH-rehsh
bandage	**penso**	PAYN-soo

Finding a cure:

I am sick.	**Estou doente.**	ish-TOH doo-AYN-teh
I need a doctor...	**Preciso de um médico...**	preh-SEE-zoo deh oo<u>n</u> MEH-dee-koo
...who speaks English.	**...que fale inglês.**	keh FAH-leh een-GLAYSH
It hurts here.	**Doi aqui.**	doy ah-KEE
I'm allergic to...	**Sou alérgico[a] a...**	soh ah-LEHR-zhee-koo ah
...penicillin.	**...penecilina.**	peh-neh-see-LEE-nah
I am diabetic.	**Sou diabético[a].**	soh dee-ah-BEH-tee-koo
This is serious.	**Isto é grave.**	EESH-too eh GRAH-veh
I have...	**Tenho...**	TAYN-yoo
...a burn.	**...uma queimadura.**	OO-mah kay-mah-DOO-rah
...chest pains.	**...uma dor no peito.**	OO-mah dor noo PAY-too
...a cold.	**...uma constipação.**	OO-mah kohnsh-tee-pah-SO<u>W</u>
...constipation.	**...prisão de ventre.**	pree-ZO<u>W</u> deh VAYN-treh
...a cough.	**...uma tosse.**	OO-mah TAW-seh
...diarrhea.	**...diarreia.**	dee-ah-RAY-ah
...a fever.	**...febre.**	FEH-breh
...the flu.	**...uma gripe.**	OO-mah GREE-peh

...the giggles.	...muitas guargalhadas.	MWEEN-tahsh gwar-gahl-YAH-dahsh
...a headache.	...uma dor de cabeça.	OO-mah dor deh kah-BEH-sah
...indigestion.	...uma indigestão.	OO-mah een-dee-zhish-TOW
...an infection.	...uma infecção.	OO-mah een-fehk-SOW
...nausea.	...tonturas.	tohn-TOO-rahsh
...a rash.	...uma erupção.	OO-mah ee-roop-SOW
...a sore throat.	...uma dor de garganta.	OO-mah dor deh gar-GAHN-tah
...a stomach ache.	...uma dor de estômago.	OO-mah dor deh ish-TOH-mah-goo
...a swelling.	...um inchado.	oon een-SHAH-doo
...a toothache.	...uma dor de dente.	OO-mah dor deh DAYN-teh
...a venereal disease.	...uma doença venéria.	OO-mah doo-AYN-sah veh-NEH-ree-ah
...worms.	...vermes.	VEHR-mehsh
I have body odor.	Tenho cheiro corporal.	TAYN-yoo SHAY-roo kor-poo-RAHL
Is it serious?	Isto é grave?	EESH-too eh GRAH-veh

Help!

Help in general:

Help!	**Socorro!**	soo-KOH-roo
Help me!	**Ajude-me!**	ah-ZHOO-deh-meh
Call a doctor!	**Chame um médico!**	SHAH-meh oon MEH-dee-koo
ambulance	**ambulância**	ahm-boo-LAHN-see-ah
accident	**acidente**	ah-see-DAYN-teh
injured	**ferido**	feh-REE-doo
emergency	**emergência**	ee-mehr-ZHAYN-see-ah
fire	**fogo**	FOH-goo
police	**polícia**	poo-LEE-see-ah
thief	**ladrão**	lah-DROW
pick-pocket	**carteirista**	kar-tay-REESH-tah
I've been ripped off.	**Fui roubado[a].**	fwee roh-BAH-doo
I've lost...	**Perdi...**	PEHR-dee
...my passport.	**...o meu passaporte.**	oo MEH-oo pah-sah-POR-teh
...my ticket.	**...o meu bilhete.**	oo MEH-oo beel-YEH-teh
...my baggage.	**...as minhas malas.**	ahsh MEEN-yahsh MAH-lahsh
...my purse.	**...a minha bolsa.**	ah MEEN-yah BOHL-sah

...my wallet.	...a minha carteira.	ah MEEN-yah kar-TAY-rah
...my faith in humankind.	...a minha fé na humanidade.	ah MEEN-yah feh nah oo-mah-nee-DAH-deh
I'm lost.	Estou perdido[a].	ish-TOH pehr-DEE-doo

Help for women:

Leave me alone.	Deixe-me em paz.	DAY-sheh-meh ayn pahsh
I wish to be alone.	Quero estar sózinha.	KEH-roo ish-TAR saw-ZEEN-yah
I'm not interested.	Não estou interessada.	now ish-TOH een-teh-reh-SAH-dah
I'm married.	Sou casada.	soh kah-ZAH-dah
I'm a lesbian.	Sou lésbia.	soh LEHZH-bee-ah
I have a contagious disease.	Tenho uma doença contagiosa.	TAYN-yoo OO-mah doo-AYN-sah kohn-tah-zhee-OH-zah
Stop following me.	Pare de me seguir.	PAH-reh deh meh seh-GEER
Don't touch me.	Não me toque.	now meh TAW-keh
Enough!	Chega!	SHAY-gah
Get lost!	Desapareça!	day-zah-pah-RAY-sah
Drop dead!	Quero que morra!	KEH-roo keh MOR-rah
I'll call the police!	Vou chamar a polícia!	voh shah-MAR ah poo-LEE-see-ah
Police!	Polícia!	poo-LEE-see-ah

Conversations

Getting to know you:

My name is...	**Chamo-me...**	SHAH-moo-meh
What's your name?	**Como se chama?**	KOH-moo seh SHAH-mah
How are you?	**Como está?**	KOH-moo ish-TAH
Very well, thank you.	**Muito bem, obrigado[a].**	MWEEN-too bayn oh-bree-GAH-doo
I am... / You are...	**Estou... / Está...**	ish-TOH / ish-TAH
...happy.	**...contente.**	kohn-TAYN-teh
...sad.	**...triste.**	TREESH-teh
...tired.	**...cansado[a].**	kahn-SAH-doo
...thirsty.	**...com sede.**	kohn SAY-deh
...hungry.	**...com fome.**	kohn FAW-meh
..lucky.	**...afortunado[a].**	ah-for-too-NAH-doo
...cold.	**...com frio.**	kohn FREE-oh
I don't smoke.	**Não fumo.**	now FOO-moo
Where are you from?	**De onde é que você é?**	deh OHN-deh eh keh voh-SAY eh
What city?	**De que cidade?**	deh keh see-DAH-deh
What country?	**De que pais?**	deh keh pah-EESH
What planet?	**De que planeta?**	deh keh plah-NAY-tah
I am American.	**Sou Americano[a].**	soh ah-meh-ree-KAH-noo

I am Canadian.	**Sou Canadiano[a].**	soh kah-nah-dee-AH-noo
(This is) my...	**O meu...**	oo MEH-oo
...male friend.	**...amigo.**	ah-MEE-goo
...boyfriend.	**...namorado.**	nah-moo-RAH-doo
...husband.	**...marido.**	mah-REE-doo
...son.	**...filho.**	FEEL-yoo
...brother.	**...irmão.**	eer-MO<u>W</u>
...father.	**...pai.**	pī
(This is) my...	**A minha...**	ah MEEN-yah
...female friend.	**...amiga.**	ah-MEE-gah
...girlfriend.	**...namorada.**	nah-moo-RAH-dah
...wife.	**...mulher.**	mool-YEHR
...daughter.	**...filha.**	FEEL-yah
...sister.	**...irmã.**	eer-MAH
...mother.	**...mãe.**	may

Family, school, and work:

Are you married? (asked of a man)	**É casado?**	eh kah-ZAH-doo
Are you married? (asked of a woman)	**É casada?**	eh kah-ZAH-dah
Do you have children?	**Tem algumas crianças?**	tay<u>n</u> ahl-GOO-mahsh kree-AHN-sahsh
Do you have photos?	**Tem fotografias?**	tay<u>n</u> foo-too-grah-FEE-ahsh

How old is your child?	**Que idade tem a sua criança?**	keh ee-DAH-deh tayn ah SOO-ah kree-AHN-sah
Beautiful child!	**Linda criança!**	LEEN-dah kree-AHN-sah
Beautiful children!	**Lindas crianças!**	LEEN-dahsh kree-AHN-sahsh
What are you studying?	**O que é que está a estudar?**	oo keh eh keh ish-TAH ah ish-too-DAR
How old are you?	**Que idade tem?**	keh ee-DAH-deh tayn
I'm... years old.	**Tenho... de idade.**	TAYN-yoo... deh ee-DAH-deh
Do you have brothers and sisters?	**Tem irmãos e irmãs?**	tayn eer-MOWSH ee eer-MAHSH
What is your occupation?	**Qual é a sua profissão?**	kwahl eh ah SOO-ah proo-fee-SOW
I'm a...	**Sou...**	soh
...student.	**...estudante.**	ish-too-DAHN-teh
...teacher.	**...professor[a].**	proo-feh-SOR
...worker.	**...trabalhador[a].**	trah-bahl-yah-DOR
...brain surgeon.	**...cirurgião de cérebro.**	see-roor-ZHOW deh SEH-reh-broo
...professional traveler.	**...viajante professional.**	vee-ah-ZHAHN-teh proo-feh-see-oo-NAHL
Do you like your work?	**Gosta do seu trabalho?**	GAWSH-tah doo SEH-oo trah-BAHL-yoo

Travel talk:

Are you on vacation?	**Está de férias?**	ish-TAH deh FEH-ree-ahsh
A business trip?	**Uma viagem de negócios?**	OO-mah vee-AH-zhayn deh neh-GAW-see-oosh
How long have you been traveling?	**Á quanto tempo é que tem estado a viajar?**	ah KWAHN-too TAYN-poo eh keh tayn ish-TAH-doo ah vee-ah-ZHAR
day / week	**dia / semana**	DEE-ah / seh-MAH-nah
month / year	**mês / ano**	maysh / AH-noo
When are you going home?	**Quando é que vai voltar para casa?**	KWAHN-doo eh keh vī vool-TAR PAH-rah KAH-zah
This is my first time in...	**Esta é a minha primeira vez...**	EHSH-tah eh ah MEEN-yah pree-MAY-rah vaysh
I've visited... and then...	**Visitei... e depois...**	vee-zee-TAY... ee deh-POYSH
Today / Tomorrow I'll go to...	**Hoje / Amanhã vou para...**	OH-zheh / ah-ming-YAH voh PAH-rah
I'm homesick.	**Estou com saudades de casa.**	ish-TOH kohn soh-DAH-dehsh deh KAH-zah
I'm very happy here.	**Estou muito contente aqui.**	ish-TOH MWEEN-too kohn-TAYN-teh ah-KEE

The Portuguese are very friendly.	**Os Portugueses são muito simpáticos.**	oosh por-too-GAY-zehsh sow MWEEN-too seem-PAH-tee-koosh
Portugal is a wonderful country.	**Portugal é um país maravilhoso.**	poor-too-GAHL eh oon pah-EESH mah-rah-veel-YOH-zoo
To travel is to live.	**A maneira de viver é viajar.**	ah mah-NAY-rah deh vee-VEHR eh vee-ah-ZHAR

Weather:

What will the weather be like tomorrow?	**Qual é o tempo para amanhã?**	kwahl eh oo TAYN-poo PAH-rah ah-ming-YAH
sunny / rainy	**sol / chuva**	sawl / SHOO-vah
hot / cold	**quente / frio**	KAYN-teh / FREE-oo

Favorite things:

What's your favorite...?	**Qual é o seu... favorito?**	kwahl eh oo SEH-oo... fah-voo-REE-too
...hobby	**...passatempo**	pah-sah-TAYN-poo
...ice cream	**...gelado**	zheh-LAH-doo
...male singer	**...cantor**	kahn-TOR
...male author	**...autor**	ow-TOR
...male movie star	**...actor**	ah-TOR
...movie	**...filme**	FEEL-meh
...sport	**...desporto**	dish-POR-too

...vice	...vício	VEE-see-oo
What's your favorite...?	Qual é a sua... favorita?	kwahl eh ah SOO-ah... fah-voo-REE-tah
...art	...arte	AR-teh
...music	...música	MOO-zee-kah
...female singer	...cantora	kahn-TOH-rah
...female author	...autora	ow-TOH-rah
...female movie star	...actriz	ah-TREESH

Responses for all occasions:

I like that.	Gosto disto.	GAWSH-too DEESH-too
I like you.	Gosto de ti.	GAWSH-too deh tee
You are...	Você é...	voh-SAY eh
...kind.	...simpático[a].	seem-PAH-tee-koo
...wonderful.	...maravilhoso[a].	mah-rah-veel-YOH-zoo
...generous.	...generouso[a].	zheh-neh-ROH-zoo
You've been a great help.	Você foi uma grande ajuda.	voh-SAY foy OO-mah GRAHN-deh ah-ZHOO-dah
Fantastic!	Fantástico!	fahn-TAHSH-tee-koo
Perfect.	Perfeito.	pehr-FAY-too
Funny.	Cómico.	KAW-mee-koo
Very interesting.	Muito interessante.	MWEEN-too een-teh-reh-SAHN-teh
Really?	A sério?	ah SEH-ree-oo
Wow!	Fiche!	FEE-sheh

Congratulations!	**Parabéns!**	pah-rah-BAYNSH
You're welcome.	**Não tem de quê.**	now tayn deh kay
Bless you! (after sneeze)	**Santinho!**	sahn-TEEN-yoo
What a pity!	**É uma pena!**	eh OO-mah PAY-nah
No problem.	**Não tem problema.**	now tayn proo-BLAY-mah
O.K.	**Está bem.**	ish-TAH bayn
That's life.	**É a vida.**	eh ah VEE-dah
This is the good life!	**Esta é a boa vida!**	EHSH-tah eh ah BOH-ah VEE-dah
Have a good trip!	**Boa-viagem!**	boh-ah-vee-AH-zhayn
Good luck!	**Boa-sorte!**	boh-ah-SOR-teh
Let's go!	**Vamos!**	VAH-moosh

Conversing with Portuguese animals:

rooster / cock-a-doodle-doo	**galo / co-coro-cocó**	GAH-loo / koo-koo-roo-koo-KAW
bird / tweet tweet	**pássaro / piu piu**	PAH-sah-roo / pee-OO pee-OO
cat / meow	**gato / miau**	GAH-too / MEE-ow
dog / woof woof	**cão / ão ão**	kow / ow ow
duck / quack quack	**pato / quac quac**	PAH-too / kwahk kwahk
cow / moo	**vaca / moo**	VAH-kah / moo
pig / oink oink	**porco / orn orn (or just snort)**	POR-koo / orn orn (or just snort)

Politics and Philosophy

With these lists, you can have deep (or ridiculous) political conversations with the locals.

Who:

politicians	**políticos**	poo-LEE-tee-koosh
big business	**negócio grande**	neh-GAW-see-oo GRAHN-deh
mafia	**máfia**	MAH-fee-ah
military	**militares**	mee-lee-TAH-rehsh
facists	**facista**	fah-SEESH-tah
the system	**o sistema**	oo seesh-TEH-mah
the rich	**o rico**	oo REE-koo
the poor	**o pobre**	oo PAW-breh
men / women	**homens / mulheres**	AW-maynsh / mool-YEH-rehsh
children	**crianças**	kree-AHN-sahsh
the Portuguese	**os Portugueses**	oosh poor-too-GAY-zehsh
the Spanish	**os Espanhóis**	oosh ish-pahn-YOYSH
the French	**os Franceses**	oosh frahn-SAY-zehsh
the Germans	**os Alemães**	oosh ah-leh-MAYNSH
the Americans	**os Americanos**	oosh ah-meh-ree-KAH-noosh
I / you	**eu / você**	EH-oo / voh-SAY

| everyone | **todas as** | TOH-dahsh ahsh |
| | **pessoas** | peh-SOH-ahsh |

What:

want	**querer**	keh-REHR
need	**precisar**	preh-see-ZAR
take / give	**tirar / dar**	tee-RAR / dar
prosper	**prósperar**	prawsh-peh-RAR
suffer	**sofrer**	soof-REHR
love / hate	**amar / odiar**	ah-MAR / oo-dee-AR
work	**trabalhar**	trah-bahl-YAR
play	**jogar**	zhoo-GAR
vote	**votar**	voo-TAR

Why:

love / sex	**amor / sexo**	ah-MOR / SEHK-soo
money	**dinheiro**	deen-YAY-roo
power	**poder**	poo-DEHR
family	**familia**	fah-MEEL-yah
work	**trabalho**	trah-BAHL-yoo
food	**comida**	koo-MEE-dah
health	**saúde**	sah-OO-deh
hope	**esperança**	ish-peh-RAHN-sah
religion	**religião**	ray-lee-ZHOW
happiness	**felicidade**	feh-lee-see-DAH-deh
recreational	**drogas leves**	DRAW-gahsh
drugs		LEH-vehsh
democracy	**democracia**	deh-moo-krah-SEE-ah

taxes	**taxas**	TAHSH-ahsh
lies	**mentiras**	mayn-TEE-rahsh
corruption	**corrupção**	koo-roop-SO<u>W</u>
racism	**racismo**	rah-SEESH-moo
pollution	**poluição**	pool-wee-SO<u>W</u>
war / peace	**guerra / paz**	GEH-rah / pahsh

You be the judge:

(not) important	**(não) importante**	(no<u>w</u>) eem-poor-TAHN-teh
(not) powerful	**(não) poderoso**	(no<u>w</u>) poo-deh-ROH-zoo
(not) honest	**(não) honesto**	(no<u>w</u>) oo-NEHSH-too
(not) innocent	**(não) inocente**	(no<u>w</u>) ee-noo-SAYN-teh
(not) greedy	**(não) ganan-cioso**	(no<u>w</u>) gah-nah-see-OH-zoo
liberal	**liberal**	lee-beh-RAHL
conservative	**conservador**	kohn-sehr-vah-DOR
radical	**radical**	rah-dee-KAHL
too much	**demasiado**	deh-mah-zee-AH-doo
enough	**suficiente**	soo-fee-see-AYN-teh
never enough	**nunca é suficiente**	NOON-kah eh soo-fee-see-AYN-teh
same	**mesmo**	MEHZH-moo
better / worse	**melhor / pior**	mil-YOR / pee-OR
good / bad	**bom / mau**	boh<u>n</u> / mow
here	**aqui**	ah-KEE
everywhere	**em toda parte**	ay<u>n</u> TOH-dah PAR-teh

Assorted beginnings and endings:

I (don't) like...	Eu (não) gosto...	EH-oo (now) GAWSH-too
Do you like...?	Você gosta...?	voh-SAY GAWSH-tah
I am... / Are you...?	Eu sou... / Você é...?	EH-oo soh / voh-SAY eh
I (don't) believe...	(Não) acredito...	(now) ah-kreh-DEE-too
Do you believe...?	Você acredita...?	voh-SAY ah-kreh-DEE-tah
...in God	...em Deus	ayn DEH-oosh
...in reincarnation	...em reincarnação	ayn ray-een-kar-nah-SOW
...in extra-terrestrial life	...que existe vida em outros planetas	keh ee-ZEESH-teh VEE-dah ayn OH-troosh plah-NAY-tahsh
...in Clinton	...em Clinton	ayn "Clinton"
Yes. / No.	Sim. / Não.	seeng / now
Maybe. / I don't know.	Talvez. / Não sei.	TAHL-vaysh / now say
What's most important in life?	O que é a coisa mais importante na vida?	oo keh eh ah KOY-zah mīsh eem-poor-TAHN-teh nah VEE-dah
The problem is...	O problema é...	oo proo-BLAY-mah eh
The answer is...	A resposta é...	ah rish-POHSH-tah eh
We have solved the world's problems.	Nós resolvemos os problemas do mundo.	nawsh reh-zool-VAY-moosh oosh proo-BLAY-mahsh doo MOON-doo

Entertainment

What's happening:

movie	**filme**	FEEL-meh
...original version	**...versão**	vehr-SOW
	original	oo-ree-zhee-NAHL
...in English	**...em inglês**	ayn een-GLAYSH
...with subtitles	**...com legendas**	kohn leh-ZHEHN-dahsh
...dubbed	**...dobrado**	doo-BRAH-doo
music...	**música**	MOO-zee-kah
...classical	**...clássico**	KLAH-see-koo
...folk	**...folclore**	fool-KLAW-reh
...live	**...ao vivo**	ow VEE-voo
rock / jazz / blues	**rock / jazz / blues**	"rock" / zhaz / bloosh
singer	**cantor[a]**	kahn-TOR
concert	**concerto**	kohn-SEHR-too
show	**espetáculo**	ish-peh-TAH-koo-loo
dancing	**dança**	DAHN-sah
folk dancing	**dança**	DAHN-sah
	folclórica	fool-KLAW-ree-kah
disco	**disco**	DEESH-koo
cover charge	**entrada**	ayn-TRAH-dah
Can you recommend...?	**Pode-me recomendar...?**	PAW-deh-meh reh-koo-mayn-DAR
What's happening tonight?	**O que é que está a contecer esta noite?**	oo keh eh keh ish-TAH ah kohn-teh-SEHR EHSH-tah NOY-teh

A Portuguese Romance

Words of love:

I / me / you	**eu / mim / tu**	EH-oo / meeng / too
flirt	**namorar**	nah-moo-RAR
kiss	**beijar**	bay-ZHAR
hug	**abraçar**	ah-brah-SAR
love	**amor**	ah-MOR
make love	**fazer amor**	fah-ZEHR ah-MOR
condom	**preservativo**	preh-zehr-vah-TEE-voo
contraceptive	**contraceptivo**	kohn-trah-sehp-TEE-voo
safe sex	**sexo seguro**	SEHK-soo say-GOO-roo
sexy	**sexy**	"sexy"
romantic	**romântico**	roh-MAHN-tee-koo
my tender love	**minha ternura**	MEEN-yah tehr-NOO-rah
my darling	**meu querido (m) / minha querida (f)**	MEH-oo keh-REE-doo / MEEN-yah keh-REE-dah
my angel	**meu anjo**	MEH-oo AHN-zhoo
my soft thing	**meu fofinho (m) / minha fofinha (f)**	MEH-oo foo-FEEN-yoo / MEEN-yah foo-FEEN-yah

What's the matter?	**O que é que se passa?**	oo keh eh keh seh PAH-sah
Nothing.	**Nada.**	NAH-dah
I am...	**Sou...**	soh
...straight.	**...normal.**	nor-MAHL
...gay.	**...maricas.**	mah-REE-kahsh
...undecided.	**...indeciso[a].**	een-day-SEE-zoo
...prudish.	**...puritano[a].**	poo-ree-TAH-noo
...horney.	**...excitado[a].**	ish-shee-TAH-doo
We are on our honeymoon.	**Nós estamos em lua de mel.**	nawsh ish-TAH-moosh ayn LOO-ah deh mehl
I have a...	**Tenho...**	TAYN-yoo
...a boyfriend.	**...um namorado.**	oon nah-moo-RAH-doo
...a girlfriend.	**...uma namorada.**	OO-mah nah-moo-RAH-dah
I am married.	**Sou casado[a].**	soh kah-ZAH-doo
I am not married.	**Não sou casado[a].**	now soh kah-ZAH-doo
I am rich and single.	**Sou solteiro[a] e rico[a].**	soh sool-TAY-roo ee REE-koo
I am lonely.	**Sinto-me só.**	SEEN-too-meh saw
I have no diseases.	**Não tenho nenhuma doença.**	now TAYN-yoo neen-YOO-mah doo-AYN-sah
I have many diseases.	**Tenho muitas doenças.**	TAYN-yoo MWEEN-tahsh doo-AYN-sahsh
Can I see you again?	**Quando é que o posso voltar a ver?**	KWAHN-doo eh keh oo PAW-soo vool-TAR ah vehr

Is this an aphrodisiac?	É isto um afrodisíaco?	eh EESH-too oon ah-froo-dee-ZEE-ah-koo
This is (not) my first time.	(Não) é a minha primeira vez.	(now) eh ah MEEN-yah pree-MAY-rah vaysh
Do you do this often?	Faz isto regularmente?	fahsh EESH-too reh-goo-lar-MAYN-teh
How's my breath?	Como é que cheiro da boca?	KOH-moo eh keh SHAY-roo dah BOH-kah
Let's just be friends.	Vamos ser só amigos.	VAH-moosh sehr saw ah-MEE-goosh
I'll pay for my share.	Pagarei somente a minha parte.	pah-gah-RAY soo-MAYN-teh ah MEEN-yah PAR-teh
Would you like a massage...?	Gostaria uma massagem...?	goosh-tah-REE-ah OO-mah mah-SAH-zhayn
...for your feet	...para os seus pés	PAH-rah oosh SEH-oosh pehsh
Why not?	Porque não?	poor-KAY now
Try it.	Expermente.	ish-pehr-MAYN-teh
It tickles.	Isso faz cócegas.	EE-soo fahsh KAW-see-gahsh
Oh my God.	Ó meu Deus.	aw MEH-oo DEH-oosh
I love you.	Eu amo-te.	EH-oo AH-moo-teh
Darling, will you marry me?	Querida, queres casar comigo?	keh-REE-dah KEH-rehsh kah-ZAR koo-MEE-goo

Rolling Rosetta Stone Word Guide

For centuries, Egyptian hieroglyphics were considered undecipherable -- until 1799, when a black slab known as the Rosetta Stone was unearthed in the Egyptian desert. By repeating identical phrases in hieroglyphics, Greek, and a newer form of Egyptian, Rosetta helped scientists break the ancient hieroglyphic code, and thus she became the world's first phrasebook.

As you roll through the Iberian peninsula, our thoroughly modern, portable Rosetta will help you decode key words in English, Spanish and Portuguese.

English	Spanish	Portuguese
	A	
above	encima	acima
accident	accidente	acidente
adaptor	adaptador	adaptador
address	dirección	endereço
adult	adulto	adulto
afraid	miedoso	medo
after	después	depois
afternoon	tarde	tarde
afterwards	después	depois
again	otra vez	outra vez
age	edad	idade
agency	agencia	agência
aggressive	agresivo[a]	agressivo[a]
agree	de acuerdo	de acordo
AIDS	SIDA	SIDA

English	Spanish	Portuguese
air-conditioned	aire acondicionado	ar condicionado
airline	línea aérea	linha aérea
air mail	correo aéreo	correio aéreo
airport	aeropuerto	aeroporto
alarm clock	despertador	despertador
alcohol	alcohol	alcool
allergic	alérgico[a]	alérgico[a]
allergies	alergias	alergias
all together	todos juntos	todos juntos
alone	solo	sozinho
always	siempre	sempre
am (to be)	soy	sou
ancestors	antepasados	antepassados
ancient	antiguo	antigo
and	y	e
angry	enfadado	chateado
animal	animal	animal
another	otro[a]	outro[a]
answer	respuesta	resposta
antibiotic	antibiótico	antibiótico
antiques	antigüedades	antiguidades
apartment	apartamento	apartamento
apology	disculpa	desculpa
appetizers	aperitivos	aperitivos
appointment	cita	apontamento
approximately	aproximadamente	aproximadamente
area	área	área
arrest	detención	detenção
arrival	llegada	chegada

English	Spanish	Portuguese
art	arte	arte
artificial	artificial	artificial
artist	artista	artista
ask	preguntar	perguntar
aspirin	aspirina	aspirina
at	a	á
autumn	otoño	outono

B

baby	niño[a]	bébé
babysitter	niñera	babysitter
backpack	mochila	mochila
bad	malo[a]	mau
baggage	equipaje	bagagem
bakery	panadería	padaria
balcony	balcón	varanda
ball	pelota	bola
Band-Aid	tirita	adesivo
bank	banco	banco
barber	barbero	barbeiro
basement	sótano	porão
basket	canasta	cesto
bath	baño	banho
bathroom	baño	casa de banho
bathtub	bañera	banheira
battery	batería	bateria
beach	playa	praia
beard	barba	barba
beautiful	bonito[a]	lindo[a]

English	Spanish	Portuguese
because	porque	porquê
bed	cama	cama
bedroom	habitación	quarto
bed sheet	sábana	lençol de cama
beef	carne de vaca	bife
beer	cerveza	cerveja
before	antes	antes
begin	comenzar	começar
behind	detrás	detrás
below	abajo	abaixo
belt	cinturón	cinto
best	mejor	melhor
bicycle	bicicleta	bicicleta
big	grande	grande
bill (payment)	cuenta	conta
bird	pájaro	pássaro
birthday	cumpleaños	aniversário
bite (n)	bocado	bocado
black	negro	preto
blanket	manta	corbetor
bleed	sangrar	sangrar
blond	rubio[a]	louro[a]
blood	sangre	sangue
blue	azul	azul
boat	barco	barco
body	cuerpo	corpo
boil (v)	hervir	ferver
boiling	hervor	ferver
bomb	bomba	bomba
book	libro	livro

English	Spanish	Portuguese
book shop	librería	livraria
boots	botas	botas
border	orilla	fronteira
borrow	pedir prestado	emprestar
boss	jefe	patrão
bottle	botella	garrafa
bottom	fondo	fundo
bowl	plato hondo	tijela
box	caja	caixa
boy	chico	rapaz
bra	sujetador	soutien
bread	pan	pão
breakfast	desayuno	pequeno almoço
bridge	puente	ponte
broken	roto	partido
brother	hermano	irmão
brown	marrón	castanho
browsing	mirando	só a olhar
bucket	cubo	balde
building	edificio	prédio
bulb	bombilla	lâmpada
burn (n)	quemadura	queimadura
bus	autobús	autocarro
business	negocio	negócio
but	pero	mas
button	botón	botão
by (via)	en	via

English	Spanish	Portuguese

C

English	Spanish	Portuguese
calendar	calendario	calendário
calorie	caloría	caloria
camera	cámara	camara
camping	camping	campismo
can (v)	poder	poder
Canada	Canadá	Canadá
can opener	abridor de latas	abertor de latas
canal	canal	canal
candle	candela	vela
candy	caramelo	doce
canoe	canoa	canoa
cap	gorro	boné
captain	capitán	capitão
car	coche	carro
carafe	garrafa	garrafa
card	tarjeta	cartão
cards (deck)	naipe	cartas
careful	cuidadoso	cuidadoso
carpet	alfombra	carpete
carry	llevar	carregar
cashier	cajera	caixa
cassette	cinta	cassete
castle	castillo	castelo
cat	gato	gato
catch (v)	coger	apanhar
cathedral	catedral	catedral
cave	cueva	cave
cellar	bodega	adega

English	Spanish	Portuguese
center	centro	centro
century	siglo	século
chair	silla	cadeira
change (n)	cambio	troca
cheap	barato	barato
check	cheque	cheque
Cheers!	¡Salud!	Saúde!
cheese	queso	queijo
chicken	pollo	galinha
children	niños[as]	crianças
chin	barbilla	queixo
Chinese (adj)	chino	chinês
chocolate	chocolate	chocolate
Christmas	Navidad	Natal
church	iglesia	igreija
cigarette	cigarrillo	cigarro
cinema	cine	cinema
city	ciudad	cidade
city hall	ayuntamiento	câmara da cidade
class	clase	classe
clean (adj)	limpio	limpo
clear	claro	claro
cliff	acantilado	falésia
closed	cerrado	fechado
clothesline	cordón para ropa	linha de roupas
clothes pins	pinzas	broches
cloudy	nuboso	nebuloso
coast	costa	costa
coffee	café	café
coins	monedas	moedas

English	Spanish	Portuguese
cold (adj)	frío	frio
colors	colores	cores
comb (n)	peine	pente
come	venir	vir
comfortable	cómodo	confortável
complain	quejarse	queixar
complicated	complicado	complicado
computer	computadora	computador
concert	concierto	concerto
condom	preservativo	perservativo
conductor	conductor	condutor
congratulations	felicidades	parabéns
connection (train)	enlace	conexão
constipation	estreñimiento	constipação
cook (v)	cocinar	cozinhar
cool	fresco[a]	fresco[a]
corkscrew	sacacorchos	sacarolhas
corner	esquina	esquina
corridor	pasillo	corredor
cost	precio	preço
cot	catre	rede
cotton	algodón	algodão
cough (v)	toser	tosse
cough drops	gotas para la tos	rabuçados da tosse
country	país	país
countryside	campo	campo
cousin	primo	primo
cow	vaca	vaca
credit card	tarjeta de crédito	cartão de crédito
crowd (n)	multitud	multidão

English	Spanish	Portuguese
cry (v)	llorar	chorar
cup	taza	chávena

D

English	Spanish	Portuguese
dad	papá	pai
dance (v)	bailar	dançar
danger	peligro	perigo
dangerous	peligroso	perigoso
dark	oscuro	escuro
darling	querido[a]	querido[a]
daughter	hija	filha
day	día	dia
dead	muerto[a]	morto[a]
delay	retraso	atraso
delicious	delicioso	delicioso
dental floss	hilo dental	fio dental
dentist	dentista	dentista
deodorant	desodarante	desodorizante
departure	salida	partida
deposit	depósito	depósito
dessert	postre	sobremesa
detour	desvío	desvio
diabetic	diabético	diabético
diamond	diamante	diamante
diarrhea	diarrea	diarreia
dictionary	diccionario	dicionário
difficult	difícil	difícil
dinner	cena	jantar
direct	directo	directo

English	Spanish	Portuguese
direction	dirección	direção
dirty	sucio	sujo
discount	descuento	desconto
disease	enfermedad	doença
disturb	molestar	incomudar
divorced	divorciado[a]	divorciado[a]
doctor	doctor	doutor
document	documento	documento
dog	perro	cão
doll	muñeca	boneca
donkey	burro	burro
door	puerta	porta
dormitory	dormitorio	dormitorio
double	doble	dobrar
down	abajo	abaixo
dream (n)	sueño	sonho
dress (n)	vestido	vestido
drink (n)	bebida	bebida
drive (v)	conducir	conduzir
driver	conductor	condutor
drunk	borracho	bêbado
dry	seco	seco

E

English	Spanish	Portuguese
each	cada	cada
ear	oreja	orelha
early	temprano	cedo
earplugs	tapón de oidos	tampões de ouvido
earrings	pendientes	brincos

English	Spanish	Portuguese
earth	tierra	terra
east	este	este
Easter	Pascua	Pascoa
easy	fácil	fácil
eat	comer	comer
elbow	codo	cotovelo
elevator	ascensor	elevador
embarrassing	embarazoso	humilhante
embassy	embajada	embaixada
empty	vacío	vazio
English	inglés	inglês
enough	suficiente	suficiente
entrance	entrada	entrada
envelope	sobre	envelope
Europe	Europa	Europa
evening	la tarde	noitecer
every	todo	todo
everything	todo	tudo
exactly	exactamente	exactamente
example	ejemplo	exemplo
excellent	excelente	excelente
except	excepto	excepto
exchange (n)	cambio	câmbio
excuse me	lo siento	desculpe
exhausted	agotado[a]	esgotado[a]
exit	salida	saída
expensive	caro	caro
explain	explicar	explicar
eye	ojo	olho

English	Spanish	Portuguese

F

English	Spanish	Portuguese
face	cara	cara
factory	fábrica	fábrica
fall (v)	caer	cair
false	falso[a]	falso[a]
family	familia	familia
famous	famoso[a]	famoso[a]
fantastic	fantástico[a]	fantástico[a]
far	lejos	longe
farm	granja	quinta
fashion	moda	moda
fat (adj)	gordo[a]	gordo[a]
father	padre	pai
faucet	grifo	torneira
ferry	transbordador	barco
festival	festival	festival
fever	fiebre	fevre
few	poco	pouco
field	campo	campo
fight (n)	pelea	luta
fine	fino[a]	fino[a]
finger	dedo	dedo
finish (v)	terminar	terminar
fireworks	fuegos artificiales	fogo de artificio
first	primero	primeiro
first aid	primeros auxilios	pronto socorro
first class	primera clase	primeira classe
fish	pescado	peixe
fix (v)	arreglar	arranjar

English	Spanish	Portuguese
fizzy	gaseoso	com gás
flag	bandera	bandeira
flashlight	linterna	lanterna a pilhas
flavor (n)	sabor	sabor
flea	pulga	pulga
flight	vuelo	voo
flower	flor	flor
flu	gripe	gripe
food	comida	comida
foot	pie	pé
football	fútbol	futebol
for	para	para
forbidden	prohibido	proibido
foreign	extranjero	estranjeiro
forget	olvidar	esquecer
fork	tenedor	garfo
fountain	fuente	fonte
France	Francia	França
free (no cost)	gratis	grátis
fresh	fresco[a]	fresco[a]
Friday	viernes	sexta-feira
friend	amigo[a]	amigo[a]
friendship	amistad	amizade
from	de	de
fruit	fruta	fruta
full (no vacancy)	completo	cheio
full (not empty)	lleno	cheio
fun	diversión	divertido
funeral	funeral	funeral
funny	divertido	divertido

English	Spanish	Portuguese
furniture	muebles	mobilias
future	futuro	futuro

G

English	Spanish	Portuguese
gallery	galería	galeria
game	juego	jogo
garage	garaje	garagem
garden	jardín	jardim
gas	gas	gás
gas station	gasolinera	bomba de gasolina
gay	homosexual	homosexual
gentleman	caballeros	cavalheiro
genuine	auténtico	genuíno
Germany	Alemania	Alemanha
get off	bajar	sair
get out	salir	sair
gift	regalo	prenda
girl	chica	rapariga
give	dar	dar
glass	vaso	copo
glasses (eye)	gafas	ocúlos
gloves	guantes	luvas
go	ir	ir
go away	marcharse	ir embora
God	Dios	deus
gold	oro	ouro
golf	golf	golfe
good	bueno[a]	bom
goodbye	adiós	adeus

English	Spanish	Portuguese
go through	atravesar	atravessar
grammar	gramática	gramática
grandfather	abuelo	avô
grandmother	abuela	avó
gray	gris	cinzento
greasy	grasiento	gorduroso
great	magnífico	magnifico
Great Britain	Gran Bretaña	Grã-Bretanha
Greece	Grecia	Grécia
green	verde	verde
grocery store	supermercado	mercearia
guarantee	garantía	garantia
guest	invitados	convidados
guide	guía	uma guia
guidebook	guía	um guia
guitar	guitarra	guitarra
gun	pistola	pistola

H

English	Spanish	Portuguese
hair	pelo	cabelo
hair brush	secador de pelo	escova de cabelo
haircut	corte de pelo	corte de cabelo
hand	mano	mão
handicapped	minusvalidos	aleijados
handicrafts	artesanía	artesanato
handle (n)	tirador	puxador
handsome	guapo	bonito
happy	feliz	feliz
harbor	puerto	porto

English	Spanish	Portuguese
hard	difícil	difícil
hat	sombrero	chapéu
hate	odiar	odiar
he	él	ele
head	cabeza	cabeça
headache	dolor de cabeza	dor de cabeça
healthy	sano	saudavel
hear	oír	ouvir
heart	corazón	coração
heat (n)	calor	calor
heaven	cielo	céu
heavy	pesado	pesado
hello	hola	olá
help (n)	ayuda	ajuda
here	aquí	aqui
hi	hola	olá
high	alto	alto
highway	autopista	autoestrada
hill	colina	subida
history	historia	história
hobby	pasatiempo	passatempo
hold (v)	agarrar	agarrar
hole	agujero	buraco
holiday	festivo	feriado
homemade	hecho en casa	á moda de casa
homesick	morriña	saudade
honest	honesto	honesto
honey	miel	mel
honeymoon	luna de miel	lua de mel
horrible	horrible	horrível

English	Spanish	Portuguese
horse	caballo	cavalo
horse riding	montar a caballo	montar a cavalo
hospital	hospital	hospital
hot	calor	calor
hotel	hotel	hotel
hour	hora	hora
house wine	vino de casa	vinho da casa
how many	cuánto	quanto
how much ($)	cuánto cuesta	quanto custa
how	cómo	como
hug (v)	abrazar	abraçar
hungry	hambriento[a]	esfomeado[a]
hurry (v)	apresurarse	apressar
husband	marido	marido

I

I	yo	eu
ice cream	helado	gelado
ice	hielo	gelo
ill	enfermo[a]	doente
immediately	inmediatamente	imediatamente
important	importante	importante
imported	importado	importado
impossible	imposible	impossível
in	en	em
included	incluido	incluido
incredible	increíble	inacreditável
independent	independiente	independente
indigestion	indigestión	indigestão

English	Spanish	Portuguese
industry	industria	industria
inedible	no comestible	não comestível
information	información	informação
injured	herido	ferido
innocent	inocente	inocente
insect	insecto	insecto
inside	interior	interior
instant	instante	instante
instead	en vez de	em vez de
insurance	seguro	seguro
intelligent	inteligente	inteligente
interesting	interesante	interresante
invitation	invitación	convite
is	es	ser
island	isla	ilha
Italy	Italia	Itália
itch (n)	comezón	comichão

J

English	Spanish	Portuguese
jacket	chaqueta	casaco
jeans	vaqueros	jeans
jewelry	joyas	joalheria
job	trabajo	trabalho
jogging	footing	jogging
joke (n)	chiste	piada
journey	viaje	viagem
juice	zumo	sumo
jump	saltar	saltar

English	Spanish	Portuguese

K

keep	guardar	guardar
key	llave	chave
kill	matar	matar
kind	amable	simpático
king	rey	rei
kiss (v)	besar	beijar
kitchen	cocina	cozinha
knee	rodilla	joelho
knife	cuchillo	faca
know	saber	saber

L

ladder	escalera de mano	escada
ladies	señoras	senhoras
lake	lago	lago
lamb	cordero	cordeiro
language	lenguaje	língua
large	grande	grande
last	último	último
late	tarde	tarde
later	más tarde	mais tarde
laugh (v)	reír	rir
laundromat	lavandería	lavandaria
lawyer	abogado[a]	advogado[a]
lazy	perezoso[a]	preguiçoso[a]
leather	cuero	cabedal
left	izquierda	esquerda

English	Spanish	Portuguese
leg	pierna	perna
letter	carta	carta
library	biblioteca	biblioteca
life	vida	vida
light (not heavy)	ligero[a]	leve
light (n)	luz	luz
light bulb	bombilla	lâmpada
lighter (n)	encendedor	isqueiro
lip	labio	lábio
list	lista	lista
liter	litro	litro
little	pequeño[a]	pequeno[a]
local	local	local
lock (v)	cerrar	fechar
lock (n)	cerradura	fechadura
lockers	casilleros	armários
look	mirar	olhar
lost	perdido[a]	perdido[a]
loud	ruidoso	ruidoso
love (v)	amar	amar
lover	amante	amante
low	bajo	baixo
lower	bajo	baixo
luck	suerte	sorte
lungs	pulmones	pulmões

English	Spanish	Portuguese

M

macho	macho	macho
mad	enfadado	chateado
magazine	revista	revista
maggots	gusanos	larvas
mail (n)	correo	correio
main	principal	principal
make (v)	hacer	fazer
man	hombre	homen
manager	director	gerente
many	mucho	muito
map	mapa	mapa
market	mercado	mercado
married	casado[a]	casado[a]
matches	cerillas	fosforos
maximum	máximo	máximo
maybe	tal vez	talvez
meat	carne	carne
medicine	medicina	medicina
medium	mediano	médio
men	hombres	homens
menu	menú	ementa
message	recado	recado
metal	metal	metal
middle	medio	meio
midnight	medianoche	meia-noite
mineral water	agua mineral	água mineral
minimum	mínimo	minimo
minutes	minutos	minutos

English	Spanish	Portuguese
mirror	espejo	espelho
Miss	Señorita	Menina
misunderstanding	malentendido	mal-entendido
mix (n)	mezclado	misturar
modern	moderno	moderno
mom	mamá	mãe
moment	momento	momento
Monday	lunes	segunda-feira
money	dinero	dinheiro
month	mes	mês
monument	monumento	monumento
moon	luna	lua
more	más	mais
morning	mañana	manhã
mosquito	mosquito	mosquito
mother	madre	mãe
mother-in-law	suegra	sogra
mountain	montaña	montanha
moustache	bigote	bigode
mouth	boca	boca
movie	película	filme
Mr.	Señor	Senhor
Mrs.	Señora	Senhora
much	mucho	muito
muscle	músculo	músculo
museum	museo	museu
music	música	música
my	mi	meu

English	Spanish	Portuguese

N

English	Spanish	Portuguese
nail clipper	corta uñas	corta unhas
naked	desnudo[a]	nuo[a]
name	nombre	nome
napkin	servilleta	guardanapo
narrow	estrecho	estreito
nationality	nacionalidad	nacionalidade
natural	natural	natural
nature	naturaleza	natureza
nausea	náusea	náusea
near	cerca	perto
necessary	necesario	necessário
necklace	collar	fio
needle	aguja	agulha
nervous	nervioso[a]	nervoso[a]
never	nunca	nunca
new	nuevo	novo
newspaper	periódico	jornal
next	siguiente	próximo
nice	amable	simpático
nickname	apodo	alcunha
night	noche	noite
no	no	não
noisy	ruidoso	barulho
non-smoking	no fumadores	não fumador
noon	mediodía	meio-dia
normal	normal	normal
north	norte	norte
nose	nariz	nariz

English	Spanish	Portuguese
not	no	não
notebook	cuaderno	caderno
nothing	nada	nada
no vacancy	completo	cheio
now	ahora	agora

O

English	Spanish	Portuguese
occupation	oficio	profissão
occupied	ocupado	ocupado
ocean	océano	oceano
of	de	de
office	oficina	escritório
oil (n)	aceite	azeite
O.K.	vale	O.K.
old	viejo[a]	velho[a]
on	sobre	sobre
once	una vez	uma vez
one way (street)	dirección única	sentido único
one way (ticket)	de ida	uma ida
only	sólo	só
open (adj)	abierto	aberto
open (v)	abrir	abrir
opera	ópera	ópera
operator	telefonista	operador
or	o	ou
orange (color)	naranja	cor de laranja
orange (fruit)	naranja	laranja
original	original	original
other	otro[a]	outro[a]

English	Spanish	Portuguese
oven	horno	forno
over (finished)	terminado	acabado
owner	dueño[a]	dono[a]

P

English	Spanish	Portuguese
package	paquete	embalagem
page	página	página
pail	cubo	balde
pain	dolor	dor
painting	pintura	pintura
palace	palacio	palácio
panties	bragas	cuecas
pants	pantalones	calças
paper	papel	papel
parents	padres	pais
park (v)	aparcar	estacionar
park (garden)	parque	parque
party	fiesta	festa
passenger	pasajero	passageiro
passport	pasaporte	passaporte
pay (v)	pagar	pagar
peace	paz	paz
pedestrian	peatón	peão
pen	bolígrafo	caneta
pencil	lápiz	lápis
people	gente	pessoas
percent	porciento	percento
perfect	perfecto	perfeito
perfume	perfume	perfume

English	Spanish	Portuguese
period (of time)	período	período
period (woman's)	regla	menstruação
person	persona	pessoa
pharmacy	farmacia	farmácia
photo	foto	fotografia
pick-pocket	carterista	carteirista
picnic	picnic	piquenique
piece	pedazo	pedaço
pig	cerdo	porco
pill	píldora	comprimido
pillow	almohada	almofada
pin	alfiler	alfinete
pink	rosa	cor de rosa
pity, it's a	que lástima	que pena
pizza	pizza	pizza
plane	avión	avião
plain	al natural	simples
plant	planta	planta
plastic	plástico	plástico
plastic bag	bolsa de plástico	saco plástico
plate	plato	prato
platform (train)	andén	cais
play (v)	jugar	jogar
please	por favor	por favor
pliers	alicates	alicate
pocket	bolsillo	bolso
point (v)	apuntar	apontar
police	policía	polícia
poor	pobre	pobre
pork	cerdo	porco

English	Spanish	Portuguese
Portugal	Portugal	Portugal
possible	posible	possível
postcard	carta postal	cartão postal
poster	cartel	poster
pot	olla	vaso
practical	práctico	prático
pregnant	embarazada	grávida
prescription	prescripción	receita médica
present (gift)	regalo	presente
pretty	bonito[a]	bonito[a]
price	precio	preço
priest	sacerdote	padre
private	privado	privado
problem	problema	problema
prohibited	prohibido	proibido
pronounce	pronunciar	pronunciar
public	público	público
pull	tirar	tirar
purple	morado	roxo
purse	bolso	bolsa
push	empujar	empurrar

Q

English	Spanish	Portuguese
quality	calidad	qualidade
quarter (¼)	cuarta parte	quarto
queen	reina	rainha
question (n)	pregunta	pergunta
quiet	tranquilo[a]	calado[a]

English	Spanish	Portuguese

R

English	Spanish	Portuguese
rabbit	conejo	coelho
radio	radio	rádio
railway	ferrocarril	caminho de ferro
rain (n)	lluvia	chuva
rainbow	arco iris	arco íris
raincoat	impermeable	casaco impermeável
rape (n)	violación	violação
raw	crudo	cru
razor	Gilete	Gilete
ready	listo	pronto
receipt	recibo	recibo
receive	recibir	receber
receptionist	recepcionista	recepcionista
recipe	receta	receita
recommend	recomendar	recomendar
red	rojo	vermelho
refund (n)	reembolso	reembolso
relax	relajar	relaxar
religion	religión	religião
remember	recordar	recordar
rent (v)	alquilar	renda
repair	arreglar	reparar
repeat	repetir	repetir
reservation	reserva	reserva
rich	rico[a]	rico[a]
right (direction)	derecha	direita
right (correct)	correcto	certo
ring (n)	sortija	campaínha

English	Spanish	Portuguese
ripe	maduro[a]	maduro[a]
river	río	rio
rock (n)	roca	rock
roller skates	patines	patins
romantic	romántico	romântico
roof	techo	telhado
room	habitación	quarto
rope	cuerda	corda
rotten	podrido[a]	podre
roundtrip	ida y vuelta	ida e volta
rowboat	bote	barco de passeio
rucksack	mochila	mochila
rug	alfombra	carpete
ruins	ruinas	ruínas
run (v)	correr	correr

S

English	Spanish	Portuguese
sad	triste	triste
safe	fuera de peligro	seguro
sale	rebajas	saldos
same	mismo[a]	mesmo[a]
sandals	sandalias	sandálias
sandwich	bocadillo	sande
sanitary napkins	toallas sanitarias	pensos higiénicos
Saturday	sábado	sábado
scandalous	escandaloso	escandulo
school	colegio	escola
science	ciencia	ciência
scissors	tijeras	tesouras

English	Spanish	Portuguese
scream (v)	chillar	gritar
screwdriver	destornillador	chave de parafusos
sculptor	escultor	escultor
sculpture	escultura	escultura
sea	mar	mar
seafood	marisco	marisco
seat	asiento	lugar, assento
second class	segunda clase	segunda classe
secret	secreto	segredo
see	ver	ver
self-service	auto-servicio	auto serviço
sell	vender	vender
send	enviar	enviar
separate	separado	separado
serious	serio	sério
service	servicio	serviço
sex	sexo	sexo
sexy	sexy	sexy
shampoo	champú	xampú
shaving cream	espuma de afeitar	creme de barbear
she	ella	ela
sheet	sábana	lençol
shell	concha	concha
ship (n)	barco	barco
shirt	camisa	camisa
shoes	zapatos	sapatos
shopping	compras	compras
shore	orilla	costa
short	corto	curto
shorts	pantalones cortos	calções

English	Spanish	Portuguese
shoulder	hombros	ombros
show (v)	enseñar	mostrar
show (n)	espectáculo	espectáculo
shower	ducha	chuveiro
shy	tímido	tímido
sick	enfermo	doente
sign	señal	sinal
silence	silencio	silêncio
silk	seda	seda
silver	plata	prata
similar	similar	similar
simple	sencillo	simples
sing	cantar	cantar
singer	cantante	cantor
sink	lavabo	lavatório
sir	señor	senhor
sister	hermana	irmã
size	talla	tamanho
ski (v)	esquiar	esquiar
skin	piel	pele
skinny	delgado[a]	magro[a]
skirt	falda	saia
sky	cielo	céu
sleep (v)	dormir	dormir
sleepy	soñoliento[a]	com sono
slice	rodaja	fatia
slide (photo)	diapositiva	slide
slippery	resbaladizo	escorregadio
slow	despacio	devagar
small	pequeño	pequeno

English	Spanish	Portuguese
smell (n)	olor	cheiro
smile (v)	sonrisa	sorrir
smoking	fumadores	fumar
snack	bocado	petiscar
sneeze (v)	estornudar	espirro
snore (v)	roncar	ressonar
soap	jabón	sabão
socks	calcetines	meias
something	alguna cosa	alguma coisa
son	hijo	filho
song	canción	canção
soon	pronto	cedo
sorry	lo siento	infelizmente
sour	agrio[a]	azedo[a]
south	sur	sul
Spain	España	Espanha
speak	hablar	falar
speciality	especialidad	especialidade
speed	velocidad	velocidade
spend	gastar	gastar
spider	araña	arranha
spoon	cuchara	colher
sport	deporte	desporto
spring (n)	primavera	primavera
square (town)	plaza	praça
stairs	escaleras	escadas
stamp	sello	selo
star (in sky)	estrella	estrela
state	estado	estado
station	estación	estação

English	Spanish	Portuguese
stomach	estomago	estômago
stone	piedra	pedra
stop (n)	parada	parar
stop (v)	parar	parar
storm	tormenta	tempestada
story (floor)	planta	andar
straight	derecho	em frente
strange	extraño	estranho
stream (n)	arroyo	corrente
street	calle	rua
string	cuerda	fio
strong	fuerte	forte
stuck	atascado	imobilizado
student	estudiante	estudante
stupid	estúpido	estúpido
sturdy	robusto	sólido
style	estilo	estilo
subway	metro	metro
suddenly	de repente	de repente
suitcase	maleta	mala
summer	verano	verão
sun	sol	sol
sunbathe	tomar el sol	bronzear
sunburn	quemadura	queimadura solar
Sunday	domingo	domingo
sunglasses	gafas de sol	óculos de sol
sunny	soleado	sol
sunset	puesta de sol	pôr do sol
sun screen	protector solar	protector solar
sunshine	luz del sol	brilho de sol

English	Spanish	Portuguese
sunstroke	insolación	insolação
suntan (n)	bronceado	bronzeado
suntan lotion	bronceador	creme de bronzear
supermarket	supermercado	supermercado
supplement	suplemento	suplemento
surprise (n)	sorpresa	surpresa
swallow (v)	tragar	engolir
sweat (v)	sudar	suar
sweater	suéter	pullover
sweet	dulce	doce
swim	nadar	nadar
swimming pool	piscina	piscina
swim suit	traje de baño	fato de banho
swim trunks	bañador	calção de banho
Switzerland	Suiza	Suíça
synthetic	sintético	sintético

T

English	Spanish	Portuguese
table	mesa	mesa
tail	rabo	rabo
take out (food)	para llevar	para levar
take	tomar	tomar
talcum powder	polvos de talco	pó de talco
talk	hablar	falar
tall	alto	alto
tampons	tampones	tampões
tape (cassette)	casete	cassete
taste (n)	sabor	sabor
taste (try)	probar	provar

English	Spanish	Portuguese
tax	impuesto	taxa
teacher	profesor[a]	professor[a]
team	equipo	equipa
teenager	joven	jovem
telephone	teléfono	telefone
television	telivisión	televisão
temperature	temperatura	temperatura
tender	tierno	tenro
tennis shoes	tenis	sapatos de ténis
tent	tienda de campaña	tenda
terrible	terrible	terrível
thanks	gracias	obrigado
theater	teatro	teatro
thermometer	termómetro	termómetro
they	ellos[as]	eles[as]
thick	grueso	grosso
thief	ladrón	ladrão
thigh	muslo	coxa
thin	delgado[a]	magro[a]
thing	cosa	coisa
think	pensar	pensar
thirsty	sediento[a]	sede
thread	hilo	linha
throat	garganta	garganta
through	a través	através
throw	tirar	atirar
Thursday	jueves	quinta-feira
ticket	billete	bilhete
tight	apretado	apretado
timetable	horario	horário

English	Spanish	Portuguese
tired	cansado[a]	cansado[a]
tissues	pañuelo de papel	lenço de papel
to	a	para
today	hoy	hoje
toe	dedo del pie	dedo do pé
together	juntos	juntos
toilet paper	papel higiénico	papel higiénico
toilet	servicios	casa de banho
tomorrow	mañana	amanhã
tonight	esta noche	esta noite
tool	herramienta	farramenta
tooth	dientes	dentes
toothbrush	cepillo de dientes	escova de dentes
toothpaste	pasta de dientes	pasta de dentes
toothpick	palillo	palito
total	total	total
touch (v)	tocar	tocar
tough	duro	duro
tour	viaje	excursão
tourist	turista	turista
towel	toalla	toalha
tower	torre	torre
town	pueblo	cidade
toy	juguete	brinquedo
track (train)	vía	caminho de ferro
traditional	tradicional	tradicional
traffic	tráfico	tráfico
train	tren	comboio
transfer money	transferencia	transferência
translate	traducir	traduzir

English	Spanish	Portuguese
travel (v)	viajar	viajar
travel agency	agencia de viajes	agência de viagens
traveler's check	cheque de viajero	cheque de viagem
tree	árbol	árvore
trip	viaje	viagem
trouble	dificultad	problema
T-shirt	camiseta	T-shirt
Tuesday	martes	terça-feira
tunnel	túnel	túnel
turn (v)	girar	volta
tweezers	pinzas	pinsa
twins	gemelos	gêmeos

U

ugly	feo	feio
umbrella	paraguas	guarda-chuva
under	debajo	debaixo
underpants	calzoncillos	cuecas
understand	entender	entender
unemployed	sin empleo	desempregado
United States	Estados Unidos	estados unidos
university	universidad	universidade
up	arriba	subida
upper	arriba	topo
upstairs	escaleras	escadas
urgent	urgente	urgente
us	nosotros[as]	nós
use (v)	usar	usar

English	Spanish	Portuguese

V

English	Spanish	Portuguese
vacancy sign	habitaciónes	quartos
vacant	vacante	vaga
valley	valle	vale
vegetarian	vegetariano[a]	vegetariano[a]
very	muy	muito
vest	chaleco	colete
video	vídeo	vídeo
video recorder	vídeo-grabadora	câmara vídeo
view	vista	vista
village	aldea	aldeia
vineyard	viñedo	vinhedo
virus	virus	vírus
visit (n)	visita	visita
vitamins	vitaminas	vitaminas
voice	voz	voz
vomit	vomitar	vomitar

W

English	Spanish	Portuguese
waist	cintura	cintura
wait (v)	esperar	esperar
waiter	camarero	criado
waitress	camarera	senhora, menina
wake up	despertarse	acordar
walk (v)	andar	andar
wallet	cartera	carteira
want	querer	querer
warm (adj)	caliente	quente

English	Spanish	Portuguese
wash	lavar	lavar
watch (v)	vigilar	olhar
watch (n)	reloj	relógio
water	agua	água
water, tap	agua del grifo	água da torneira
waterfall	cascada	queda de água
we	nosotros[as]	nós
weather	tiempo	tempo
wedding	boda	casamento
Wednesday	miércoles	quarta-feira
week	semana	semana
weight	peso	peso
welcome	bienvenido[a]	bem-vindo[a]
west	oeste	oeste
wet	mojado	molhado
what	qué	o quê
wheel	rueda	roda
when	cuándo	quando
where	dónde	donde
white	blanco	branco
who	quién	quem
why	por qué	porquê
widow(er)	viuda[o]	viúva[o]
wife	esposa	esposa
wild	salvaje	salvagem
wind	viento	vento
window	ventana	janela
wine	vino	vinho
wing	ala	asa
winter	invierno	inverno

English	Spanish	Portuguese
wish (v)	desear	desejo
with	con	com
without	sin	sem
woman	mujer	mulher
women	mujeres	mulheres
wood	madera	madeira
wool	lana	lã
word	palabra	palavra
work (n)	trabajo	trabalho
world	mundo	mundo
worst	peor	pior
wrap (v)	envolver	embrulhar
wrist	muñeca	pulso
write	escribir	escrever

Y / Z

English	Spanish	Portuguese
year	año	ano
yellow	amarillo	amarelo
yes	si	sim
yesterday	ayer	ontem
you (formal)	usted	voçê
you (informal)	tú	tu
young	joven	novo
youth hostel	albergue de juventud	albergue de juventude
zero	cero	zero
zipper	cremallera	fecho
zoo	zoo	zoo

Hurdling the Language Barrier

Don't be afraid to communicate

Even the best phrase book won't satisfy your needs in every situation. To really hurdle the language barrier, you need to leap beyond the printed page, and dive into contact with the locals. Never, never, never allow your lack of foreign language skills to isolate you from the people and cultures you traveled halfway 'round the world to experience. Remember that in every country you visit, you're surrounded by expert, native-speaking tutors. Spend bus and train rides letting them teach you. Always start a conversation by asking politely, "Do you speak English?"

When you communicate in English with someone from another country, speak slowly, clearly, and with carefully chosen words. Use what the Voice of America calls "simple English." You're talking to people who are wishing it was written down, hoping to see each letter as it tumbles out of your mouth. Pronounce each letter, avoiding all contractions and slang. For bad examples, listen to other tourists.

Keep things caveman-simple. Make single nouns work as entire sentences ("Photo?"). Use internationally understood words ("auto kaput" works in Portugal). Butcher the language if you must. The important thing is to make the effort. To get air mail stamps, you can flap your wings and say "tweet, tweet." If you want milk, moo and pull two imaginary udders. Risk looking like a fool.

Go ahead and make educated guesses. Many situations are easy-to-fake multiple choice questions. Practice. Read timetables, concert posters and newspaper headlines. Listen to each language on a multilingual tour. Exaggerate the local accent. Self-consciousness is the deadliest communication-killer.

Choose multilingual people to communicate with, such as business people, urbanites, young well-dressed people, or anyone in the tourist trade. Use a small note pad to keep track of handy phrases you pick up, and to help you communicate more clearly with the locals by scribbling down numbers, maps, and so on. Some travelers carry important messages written on a small card (vegetarian, boiled water, your finest ice cream).

Easy cultural bugaboos to avoid
- When writing numbers, give your sevens a cross (7) and give your ones an upswing (1).
- European dates are different: Christmas is 25-12-94, not 12-25-94.
- Commas are decimal points and decimals are commas, so a dollar and a half is 1,50 and there are 5.280 feet in a mile.
- The European "first floor" is not the ground floor, but the first floor up.

International words

As our world shrinks, more and more words hop across their linguistic boundaries and become international. Savvy travelers develop a knack for choosing words most likely to be universally understood ("auto" instead of "car," "kaput" rather than "broken," "photo," not "picture"). They also internationalize their pronunciation. "University," if you play around with its sound (oo-nee-vehr-see-tay) will be understood anywhere.

Here are a few internationally understood words. Remember, cut out the Yankee accent and give each word a pan-European sound.

Stop	Kaput	Vino	Restaurant
Ciao	Bank	Hotel	Bye-bye
Rock 'n roll	Post	Camping	OK
Auto	Picnic	Amigo	Autobus (boos)
Nuclear	Macho	Tourist	"Engleesh"
Yankee	Americano	Mama mia	Michelangelo
Beer	Oo la la	Coffee	Casanova
Chocolate	Moment	Sexy	Disneyland
Tea	Coca-Cola	No problem	Mañana
Telephone	Photo	Photocopy	Passport
Europa	Self-service	Toilet	Police
Super	Taxi	Central	Information
Pardon	University	Fascist	Rambo
American profanity			

Tongue twisters:

Here are a few that are sure to challenge you and amuse your Iberian hosts.

Spanish tongue twisters:

Pablito clavó un clavito. ¿Qué clavito clavó Pablito?

Paul stuck in a stick. What stick did Paul stick in?

Un tigre, dos tigres, tres tigres comían trigo en un trigal. Un tigre, dos tigres, tres tigres.

One tiger, two tigers, three tigers ate wheat in a wheatfield. One tiger, two tigers, three tigers.

El cielo está enladrillado. ¿Quién lo desenladrillará? El desenladrillador que lo desenladrille un buen desenladrillador será.

The sky is bricked up. Who will unbrick it? He who unbricks it, what a fine unbricker he will be.

Portuguese tongue twisters:

O rato roeu a roupa do rei de Roma.

The mouse nibbled the clothes of the king of Rome.

Um tigre, dois tigres, três tigres.

One tiger, two tigers, three tigers.

Se cá nevasse fazia-se cá ski, mas como cá não neva não se faz cá ski.

If the snow would fall, we'd ski, but since it doesn't, we don't.

English tongue twisters:
After your Iberian friends have laughed at you, let
them try these tongue twisters in English.

One smart fellow he felt smart, two smart fellows they
felt smart, three smart fellows they all felt smart.

The sixth sick sheik's sixth sheep's sick.

I'm a pleasant mother pheasant plucker. I pluck
mother pheasants. I'm the most pleasant mother
peasant plucker that ever plucked a mother pheasant.

Common Iberian Gestures

The Eyelid Pull: Place your extended forefinger below the center of your eye, and pull the skin downward. In Spain this is a friendly warning, meaning "Be alert, that guy is clever."

The Fingertip Kiss: Bring the thumb and fingers of your right hand together at your lips, kiss gently, and toss them up and away. This usually means praise in Spain, and is used as a form of salutation in Portugal.

The Hand Purse: Straighten the fingers and thumb of one hand, bringing them all together to make an upward point. Your hands can be held still or moved a little up and down at the wrist. In Iberia, this means "lots."

The Cheek Screw: Make a fist, stick out your forefinger and screw it into your cheek. This is used in southern Spain to call someone "effeminate."

The Nose Flick: Thumbing your nose is used as a form of mockery in Spain and Portugal.

Hook 'em Horns: Stick out your index finger and pinky, and hold your two middle fingers down with your thumb. Either you're a Texas Longhorns fan or you're accusing someone of impotence.

The Forearm Jerk: Clench your right fist, and jerk your forearm up as you slap your bicep with your left palm. This is a rude phallic gesture that Iberians use the way Americans give someone "the finger." This extra-large version says "I'm superior."

Counting on fingers: Counting begins with the thumb, so if you hold up two fingers, someone will sell you three of something.

To beckon someone: In Iberia, wave your hand palm downward.

Let's Talk Telephones

Using Iberian telephones

Smart travelers use the telephone every day. Making a hotel reservation by phone the morning of the day you plan to arrive is a snap. If there's a language problem, ask someone at your hotel to call your next hotel for you.

The key to long distance is understanding area codes and having a local phone card. Hotel room phones are reasonable for local calls, but a terrible rip-off for long distance calls (unless you're calling the USA with your calling card's local access number).

For calls to other European countries outside Spain and Portugal, dial the international access code (09 from Spain and 00 from Portugal), followed by the country code, followed by the area code without its first zero, and finally the local number (four to seven digits). When dialing long distance within either Spain or Portugal, first dial 9 in Spain or 0 in Portugal, then the area code (including its zero), then the local number. Post offices have fair, metered long distance phone booths.

Local telephone cards are much easier to use than coins for local and long distance calls. Buy one on your first day to force you to find smart reasons to use the local phones. The phone cards cost from $4 to $8. You can buy them at post offices and tobacco shops. The older coin-operated phones work if you have the necessary pile of small change.

Calling the USA from a pay phone is easy if you have a local phone card, or an ATT, MCI or SPRINT credit card. Or you can make a short call using coins ($1 for 15 seconds) and ask the other person to call you back at your hotel at a specified time. From the States, they would dial 011, then the country code (34 for Spain or 351 for Portugal), then your Spanish or Portuguese area code (without the zero), followed by the local number. Iberia-to-USA calls are twice as expensive as direct calls from the States. Midnight in California is breakfast in Iberia.

If you plan to call home often, get an ATT, MCI or SPRINT card. Each card company has a toll-free access number in each European country which puts you in touch with an American operator who takes your card number and the number you want to call, puts you through and bills your home phone number for the call (at the cheaper USA rate of about a dollar a minute plus a $2.50 service charge). If you talk for at least 3 minutes, you'll save enough to make up for the service charge.

Important numbers:

	Spain	Portugal
Int'l access code (calling from):	09	00
Country code: (calling to)	34	351
ATT operator:	900-99-0011	05-017-1288
MCI operator:	900-99-0014	05-018-120-33
SPRINT operator:	900-99-0013	05-017-1877
Directory assistance:	009	118

Country codes:

France:	33	Germany:	49	USA/Canada:	1
Austria:	43	Britain:	44	Switzerland:	41
Belgium:	32	Spain:	34	Portugal:	351

Major Iberian area codes:

Madrid:	1	Sevilla	5	Granada:	58
Barcelona:	3	Toledo:	25	Lisbon:	1
Coimbra:	39				

Metric conversions (approximate)

1 inch = 25 millimeters	1 foot = .3 meter
1 yard = .9 meter	1 mile = 1.6 kilometers
1 sq. yard = .8 sq. meter	1 acre = 0.4 hectare
1 quart = .95 liter	1 ounce = 28 grams
1 pound = .45 kilo	1 kilo = 2.2 pounds
1 centimeter = 0.4 inch	1 meter = 39.4 inches
1 kilometer = .62 mile	36-24-36 = 90-60-90

Miles = kilometers divided by 2 plus 10%
(120 km/2 = 60, 60 +12 = 72 miles)
Fahrenheit degrees = double Celsius + 30
32° F = 0° C, 82° F = about 28° C

Weather
First line is average daily low (°F.); second line is
average daily high (°F.); third line, days of no rain.

	J	F	M	A	M	J	J	A	S	O	N	D
Madrid	33	35	40	44	50	57	62	62	56	48	40	35
	47	51	47	64	71	80	87	86	77	66	54	48
	22	19	20	21	22	24	28	29	24	23	20	22
Barcelona	42	44	47	51	57	63	69	69	65	58	50	44
	56	57	61	64	71	77	81	82	67	61	62	57
	26	21	24	22	23	25	27	26	23	23	23	25
Malaga	47	48	51	55	60	66	70	72	68	61	53	48
	61	62	64	69	74	80	84	85	81	74	67	62
	25	22	23	25	28	29	31	30	28	27	22	25
Lisbon	46	47	49	52	56	60	63	64	62	57	52	47
	56	58	61	64	69	75	79	80	76	69	62	57
	22	20	21	23	25	28	30	30	26	24	20	21
Lagos (Algarve)	47	57	50	52	56	60	64	65	62	58	52	48
	61	61	63	67	73	77	83	84	80	73	66	62
	22	19	20	24	27	29	31	31	28	26	22	22

Your tear-out cheat sheets

Keep these most essential phrases in your pocket.
Memorize them during idle moments and use them if
you're caught without your phrase book.

Spanish essentials:

Hello.	**Hola.**	OH-lah
Do you speak	**¿Habla usted**	AH-blah oos-TEHD
English?	**inglés?**	een-GLAYS
Yes.	**Sí.**	see
No.	**No.**	noh
I don't understand.	**No comprendo.**	noh kohm-PREHN-doh
I'm sorry.	**Lo siento.**	loh see-EHN-toh
Please.	**Por favor.**	por fah-BOR
Thanks.	**Gracias.**	GRAH-thee-ahs
Goodbye.	**Adiós.**	ah-dee-OHS

Where?

Where is a...?	**Donde hay un...?**	DOHN-day ī oon
...hotel	**...hotel**	oh-TEL
...restaurant	**...restaurante**	rays-toh-RAHN-tay
...grocery store	**...supermercado**	soo-pehr-mehr-KAH-doh
Where is the...?	**Dónde está la...?**	DOHN-day ays-TAH lah
...train station	**...estación de trenes**	ays-tah-thee-OHN day TRAY-nays

...tourist information office	...Oficina de Turismo	oh-fee-THEE-nah day too-REES-moh
Where are the toilets?	¿Dónde están los servicios?	DOHN-day ays-TAHN lohs sehr-BEE-thee-ohs
men / women	hombres / mujeres	OHM-brays / moo-HEH-rays

How much in Spanish?

How much does it cost?	¿Cuánto cuesta?	KWAHN-toh KWAYS-tah
Cheaper.	Más barato.	mahs bah-RAH-toh
Is it included?	¿Está incluido?	ays-TAH een-kloo-EE-doh
I would like...	Quería...	keh-REE-ah
Just a little.	Un poquito.	oon poh-KEE-toh
More.	Más.	mahs
A ticket.	Un billete.	oon bee-YEH-tay
A room.	Una habitación.	OO-nah ah-bee-tah-thee-OHN
The bill.	La cuenta.	lah KWAYN-tah
one	uno	OO-noh
two	dos	dohs
three	tres	trays
four	cuatro	KWAH-troh
five	cinco	THEEN-koh
six	seis	says
seven	siete	see-EH-tay
eight	ocho	OH-choh
nine	nueve	NWAY-bay
ten	diez	dee-AYTH

Portuguese essentials:

Hello.	**Olá.**	oh-LAH
Do you speak English?	**Fala inglês?**	FAH-lah een-GLAYSH
Yes.	**Sim.**	seeng
No.	**Não.**	no<u>w</u>
I don't understand.	**Não compreendo.**	no<u>w</u> kohm-pree-AYN-doo
I'm sorry.	**Desculpe.**	dish-KOOL-peh
Please.	**Por favor.**	poor fah-VOR
Thanks.	**Obrigado[a].**	oh-bree-GAH-doo
Goodbye.	**Adeus.**	ah-DEH-oosh

Where?

Where is...?	**Onde é que é...?**	OHN-deh eh keh eh
...a hotel	**...um hotel**	oo<u>n</u> oh-TEHL
...a restaurant	**...um restaurante**	oo<u>n</u> rish-toh-RAHN-teh
...a grocery store	**...uma mercearia**	OO-mah mehr-see-ah-REE-ah
...the train station	**...a estação de comboio**	ah ish-tah-SO<u>W</u> deh kohm-BOY-yoo
...tourist information	**...a informação turistica**	ah een-for-mah-SO<u>W</u> too-REESH-tee-kah
...the toilet	**...a casa de banho**	ah KAH-zah deh BAHN-yoo
men / women	**homens / mulheres**	AW-may<u>n</u>sh / mool-YEH-rehsh

How much in Portuguese?

How much does it cost?	**Quanto custa?**	KWAHN-too KOOSH-tah
Cheaper.	**Mais barato.**	mīsh bah-RAH-too
Is it included?	**Está incluido?**	ish-TAH een-kloo-EE-doo
I would like...	**Gostaria...**	goosh-tah-REE-ah
Just a little.	**Só um bocadinho.**	saw oon boo-kah-DEEN-yoo
More.	**Mais.**	mīsh
A ticket.	**Um bilhete.**	oon beel-YEH-teh
A room.	**Um quarto.**	oon KWAR-too
The bill.	**A conta.**	ah KOHN-tah
one	**um**	oon
two	**dois**	doysh
three	**três**	traysh
four	**quatro**	KWAH-troo
five	**cinco**	SEENG-koo
six	**seis**	saysh
seven	**sete**	SEH-teh
eight	**oito**	OY-too
nine	**nove**	NAW-veh
ten	**dez**	dehsh

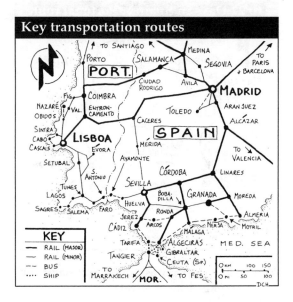

Key transportation routes

KEY
- ── RAIL (MAJOR)
- ── RAIL (MINOR)
- ‐‐ BUS
- ···· SHIP

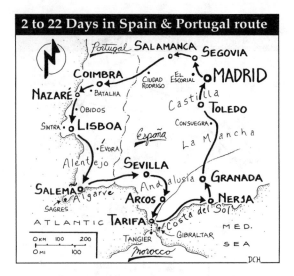

2 to 22 Days in Spain & Portugal route

You've got your phrase book, but have you planned your itinerary yet?

If this route looks good to you, pick up a copy of Rick Steves' *2 to 22 Days in Spain and Portugal*. You'll get the most productive day-by-day itinerary through the wonders of Iberia, with up-to-date listings of Rick's favorite budget accommodations along the way.

The Europe Through the Back Door Catalog

All of these items have been specially designed for independent budget travelers. They have been thoroughly field-tested by Rick Steves and his globe-trotting ETBD staff, and are completely guaranteed. Prices include shipping, tax (where applicable), and a free subscription to our quarterly newsletter/catalog.

Back Door Bag convertible suitcase/backpack $70

At 9"x21"x13" this specially-designed, sturdy, functional bag is maximum carry-on-the-plane size (fits under the seat), and your key to foot-loose and fancy-free travel. Made from rugged, water-resistant Cordura nylon, it converts from a smart-looking suitcase to a handy backpack. It has hide-away padded shoulder straps, top and side handles, and a detachable shoulder strap (for toting as a suitcase). Lockable perimeter zippers allow easy access to the roomy (2500 cubic inches) central compartment. Two large outside pockets are perfect for frequently used items. Also included is one nylon stuff bag. Over 40,000 Back Door travelers have used these bags around the world. Rick Steves helped design this bag, and lives out of it for 3 months at a time. Comparable bags cost much more. Available in black, grey, navy blue and teal green.

Eurailpasses

...cost the same everywhere, but only ETBD gives you a free 90-minute "How to get the most out of your railpass" video, free advice on your itinerary, and your choice of one of Rick Steves' "22 Day" books. No wonder why ETBD has become the second largest Eurailpass retailer in the USA. It's easy to order your pass by mail -- call 206/771-8303, and we'll send you a full description of the types of Eurailpasses available, pass prices, our unique map for comparing Eurail and pay-as-you-go rail prices, and our user-friendly Eurailpass order form.

Moneybelt $8

Absolutely required no matter where you're traveling! An ultra-light, sturdy, under-the-pants, one-size-fits-all nylon pouch, our svelte moneybelt is just the right size to carry your passport, airline tickets and traveler's checks comfortably. Made to ETBD's specifications, this moneybelt is your best defense against theft.

Prices are good through 1993. Orders will be processed within 2 weeks. For rush orders (which we process within 48 hours), please add $10. Send your check to:

Europe Through the Back Door

109 Fourth Ave. N, PO Box 2009
Edmonds, WA 98020
Phone: 206/771-8303   Fax: 206/771-0833

More travel guidebooks by Rick Steves...

Now more than ever, travelers are determined to get the most out of every mile, minute and dollar. That's what Rick's books are all about. He'll help you have a better trip **because** *you're on a budget, not in spite of it. Each of these books is published by John Muir Publications, and is available through your local bookstore, or the Europe Through the Back Door newsletter/catalog.*

Europe Through The Back Door

Now in its 11th edition, *ETBD* has given thousands of people the skills and confidence they needed to travel through the less-touristed "back doors" of Europe. You'll find chapters on packing, itinerary-planning, transportation, finding rooms, travel photography, keeping safe and healthy, plus individual chapters on Rick's 40 favorite back door discoveries. 1993 edition.

Mona Winks: Self-Guided Tours of Europe's Top Museums

Let's face it, museums can ruin a good vacation. But *Mona Winks* takes you by the hand, giving you fun and easy-to-follow self-guided tours through Europe's 20 most frightening and exhausting museums and cultural obligations. Packed with more than 200 maps and illustrations. 1993 edition.

Europe 101: History and Art for the Traveler
A lively, entertaining crash course in European history and art, *101* is the perfect way to prepare yourself for the rich cultural smorgasbord that awaits you.

2 to 22 Days in Europe
2 to 22 Days in Spain & Portugal
2 to 22 Days in Great Britain
2 to 22 Days in France
2 to 22 Days in Italy
2 to 22 Days in Germany, Austria & Switzerland
2 to 22 Days in Norway, Sweden & Denmark
Planning an itinerary can be the most difficult and important part of a trip -- and you haven't even left yet. To get you started, Rick gives you a day-by-day plan linking his favorite places in Europe, complete with maps, descriptions of sights, and recommended places to stay and eat. Some people follow a 22-day route to the letter, and others use it as a general outline. Either way, your *2 to 22 days in...* guidebook will help you structure your trip so you'll get the most out of every moment. These guides are updated every year.

Europe Through the Back Door Phrase Books:
French, Italian, German and Spanish/Portuguese
Finally, a series of phrase books written specially for the budget traveler! Each book gives you the words, phrases and easy-to-use phonetics you need.

What we do at Europe Through the Back Door

At ETBD we value travel as a powerful way to better understand and contribute to the world in which we live. Our mission at ETBD is to equip travelers with the confidence and skills necessary to travel through Europe independently, economically, and in a way that is culturally broadening. To do this, we:

- Teach budget travel seminars (often for free); Research and write guidebooks to Europe and a public television series;
- Sell Eurailpasses, our favorite guidebooks, maps,travel bags, and other travel accessories;
- Organize and lead 'Back Door' tours of Europe;
- Sponsor our Travel Resource Center in Edmonds, WA; ...and we travel a lot.

Back Door 'Best of Europe' tours

If you like our independent travel philosophy but enjoy the camaraderie and efficiency of group travel, our Back Door tours may be right up your alley. Every year we lead small, friendly, intimate 'Best of Europe in 22 Days' tours, and special regional tours of Turkey, Britain, France and other places that we especially love. For details, dates and prices, call 206/771-8303 and ask for our free newsletter/catalog.

Help improve this phrase book!

Your feedback will do a lot to improve future editions of this phrase book. To help tomorrow's travelers travel smarter, please use this page to jot down ideas, phrases, and suggestions as they hit you during your travels, and then send them to me. Thanks!

Rick Steves
Europe Through the Back Door
109 Fourth Ave. N, PO Box 2009
Edmonds, WA 98020

Other Great Travel Books by Rick Steves

Asia Through the Back Door, 4th ed., 400 pp. $16.95 (available 6/93)

Europe 101: History & Art for the Traveler, 4th ed., 372 pp. $15.95

Europe Through the Back Door, 11th ed., 432 pp. $17.95

Europe Through the Back Door Phrase Book: French, 168 pp. $4.95

Europe Through the Back Door Phrase Book: German, 168 pp. $4.95

Europe Through the Back Door Phrase Book: Italian, 168 pp. $4.95

Mona Winks: Self-Guided Tours of Europe's Top Museums, 2nd ed., 456 pp. $16.95

2 to 22 Days in Europe, 1993 ed., 288 pp. $13.95

2 to 22 Days in France, 1993 ed., 192 pp. $10.95

2 to 22 Days in Germany, Austria, & Switzerland, 1993 ed., 224 pp. $10.95

2 to 22 Days in Great Britain, 1993 ed., 192 pp. $10.95

2 to 22 Days in Italy, 1993 ed., 208 pp. $10.95

2 to 22 Days in Norway, Sweden, & Denmark, 1993 ed., 192 pp. $10.95

2 to 22 Days in Spain & Portugal, 1993 ed., 192 pp. $10.95

Kidding Around Seattle: A Young Person's Guide to the City, 64 pp. $9.95 (Ages 8 and up)

More European Travel Books Available from John Muir Publications

Great Cities of Eastern Europe, 256 pp. $16.95

Opera! The Guide to Western Europe's Great Houses, 296 pp. $18.95

22 Days Around the World, 1993 ed., 264 pp. $13.95

Understanding Europeans, 272 pp. $14.95

Undiscovered Islands of the Mediterranean, 2nd ed., 256 pp. $10.95

A Viewer's Guide to Art: A Glossary of Gods, People, and Creatures, 144 pp. $10.95

For Young Readers Traveling Abroad, Consider Our "Kidding Around" Travel Guides (Ages 8 and up)

Kidding Around London, 64 pp. $9.95

Kidding Around Paris, 64 pp. $9.95

Kidding Around Spain, 108 pp. $12.95

These are just a sampling of the many titles we have to offer. Whether you are traveling within the U.S. or around the world turn to John Muir Publications for unique travel titles to practically any location.

Call or write for our *free* catalog listing our complete selection of travel and young readers titles. All the necessary information is listed below.

Ordering Information

If you cannot find our books in your local bookstore, you can order directly from us. If you send us money for a book not yet available, we will hold your money until we can ship you the book. Your books will be sent to you via UPS (for U.S. destinations). UPS will not deliver to a P.O. Box; please give us a street address. Include $3.75 for the first item ordered and $.50 for each additional item to cover shipping and handling costs. For airmail within the U.S., enclose $4.00. All foreign orders will be shipped surface rate; please enclose $3.00 for the first item and $1.00 for each additional item. Please inquire about foreign airmail rates.

Method of Payment

Your order may be paid by check, money order, or credit card. We cannot be responsible for cash sent through the mail. All payments must be made in U.S. dollars drawn on a U.S. bank. Canadian postal money orders in U.S. dollars are acceptable. For VISA, MasterCard, or American Express orders, include your card number, expiration date, and your signature, or call (800) 888-7504. Books ordered on American Express cards can be shipped only to the billing address of the cardholder. Sorry, no C.O.D.'s. Residents of sunny New Mexico, add 6.125% tax to the total.

Address all orders and inquiries to:
John Muir Publications
P.O. Box 613
Santa Fe, NM 87504
(505) 982-4078
(800) 888-7504